DATA DRIVEN

DATA DRIVEN

HOW PERFORMANCE ANALYTICS DELIVERS EXTRAORDINARY SALES RESULTS

JENNY DEARBORN

WILEY

For general information about our other products and services, please contact our Customer Care Department within the United States at (800) 762-2974, outside the United States at (317) 572-3993 or fax (317) 572-4002.

Wiley publishes in a variety of print and electronic formats and by print-on-demand. Some material included with standard print versions of this book may not be included in e-books or in print-on-demand. If this book refers to media such as a CD or DVD that is not included in the version you purchased, you may download this material at http://book support.wiley.com. For more information about Wiley products, visit www.wiley.com.

Library of Congress Cataloging-in-Publication Data has been applied for and is on file with the Library of Congress.
ISBN 978-1-119-04312-6 (hbk)
ISBN 978-1-119-04335-5 (ebk)
ISBN 978-1-119-04336-2 (ebk)

Printed in the United States of America

10 9 8 7 6 5 4 3 2 1

To Dr. Karie Willyerd, who inspires me to push outside my comfort zone.

To my amazing husband and our awesome, crazy, brilliant kids—I love you. Thanks for eating take-out for a year while I worked on this project. I promise the next book will be less stressful for the family, but I can't promise I'll ever learn to cook.

CONTENTS

Contents

ACKNOWLEDGMENTS

I am so thankful and lucky to have assembled a team of talented professionals to support this project.

Deb Arnold—When she's not moonlighting as an overall task master, project manager, dialog extractor, logic checker, and cheerleader, Deb helps leaders to more effectively communicate their impact internally and externally through industry recognition. Deb is principle of Deb Arnold, Ink. | Spot-On Business Communications. Find her at www.debarnoldink.com.

MaryAlice Colen—Early contributor to get us over some initial stuck spots in story framework and business simulation. Find her at mcolen@birst.com.

Matt Dearborn—My brother is … awesome. Check him out at www.imdb.com/name/nm0213127/.

Michael Dowling—In collaboration with me and other members of the team, he conceptualized the format for the book and translated technical ideas into understandable prose. Find Michael at www.MichaelJDowling.com.

Sergey Feldman, Ph.D.—Subject-matter expert; reviewer of analytical models, algorithms, and logic and Henry Crawford's spirit-guide. Find Sergey at www.data-cowboys.com.

Filipe Muffoletto—A Graphics God if ever there was one. Find him at fmuffoletto@gmail.com.

Sanchita Sur—A global management consulting veteran and published author, Sanchita is the founder of Emplay, an award-winning analytics and advisory firm that helps companies drive better results by leveraging data, business savvy, and proprietary recommendation engines. She was a significant contributor to the creation of this book and has developed patent-pending "Sales DNA," "Deal DNA" and "Account DNA" algorithms for accurate sales predictions and prescriptive action plans. To learn more about Emplay, visit www.emplay.net.

PREFACE

A sales revolution is coming!

The next decade will witness a sea change in the way large and medium-size businesses manage their sales functions. Companies that fail to adapt to the new realities and adopt the new practices risk falling behind their competitors who do.

If you're a business leader of an enterprise-level corporation who shoulders some measure of responsibility for sales effectiveness, you need to know about and prepare for this coming revolution. Whether you realize it or not, you and your business are heading toward a tipping point, from which there can be no turning back. In fact, some of your best customers have likely already tipped. They are thinking about the sales process in a different and more compelling way than you have in the past. If you don't react now, you risk losing them forever.

To succeed in this new competitive environment, your company will need to revolutionize sales function management. It must learn to harness the power of data analytics, not just as a tool, but as a mindset. Gone are the days you or your sales leadership can work on intuition, gut feel, or past history. None of this is relevant in the new order.

HERE'S THE CRUX

"Big data" isn't just big, it's huge. Data analytics and predictive and prescriptive analytics aren't just buzz words. They're a new reality that you and I and everyone else in the business world must understand, embrace, wield, and inculcate into our corporate cultures. Scores of books have been written about how these powerful tools can improve sales performance. But most restrict their attention to a few discrete applications, such as reducing customer turnover (churn), identifying fraud (shrinkage), perfecting and positioning products, and improving the hiring, training, and increased time to productivity of sales reps.

These applications are very valuable, but they fail to capitalize on the full potential of data analytics to holistically transform sales effectiveness in all functional areas of an organization. This type of transformation is possible. I know it's possible, because I've taken the journey. My fellow travelers and I didn't have a map, because we were going into uncharted territories. But as we moved forward, each next step revealed itself to us in a continuous process discovery, learning, adapting, and accelerating change.

This book is a map of sorts. I wrote it so that you, too, can take this journey. My goal is to help you find the path to greater success for your company's sales organization by harnessing the power of data analytics. But like any other map, you have to know where you are going. You will need to adapt to your unique situation to fully leverage the opportunity for yourself and your organization.

SHARPEN YOUR COMPETITIVE EDGE

In this age when companies are competing on a global scale at electronic speed, maintaining a competitive advantage is increasingly difficult. In their excellent book *Competing on Analytics*,[1] Thomas Davenport and Jeanne Harris put it this way:

> *"Many of the previous bases for competition are no longer available. Unique geographical advantage doesn't matter in global competition, and protective regulation is largely gone. Proprietary technologies are rapidly copied, and breakthrough innovation in products or services seems increasingly difficult to achieve. What's left as a basis for competition is to execute your business with maximum efficiency and effectiveness, and to make the smartest business decisions possible."*

That's the kind of advantage data analytics can give you.

My insights about data analytics come not only from my own experiences of adopting and adapting to this new reality, but also from my ability to pull back the curtain on what other companies are doing. In my current role as the senior vice president, chief learning officer at SAP, the world's largest business-to-business software company, and founder of my own company, Actionable Analytics Group, I regularly consult with corporations around the world about their human capital management and talent development strategies. I see how companies on the forefront of the big data and predictive analytics revolution are using these advanced strategies to drive breakthrough business results with their internal sales

---

[1]Thomas H. Davenport & Jeanne G. Harris, *Competing on Analytics: The New Science of Winning*. Boston, MA: Harvard Business School Press, 2007, pp. 8–9.

talent. And I can say with considerable assurance that few, if any, corporations are using these tools in an integrated approach to comprehensively impact the sales cycle from start to finish.

The purpose of this book is to tell you how you can be a pioneer in this emerging field.

THE BIRTH OF A VISION

One of the perks of living in Palo Alto, California, in the heart of Silicon Valley, is that at any given social gathering you can find yourself chatting with some of the top technical minds in the world. These are people who are truly changing the game, inventing solutions that no one ever thought of before, and showing the world that they cannot live without them. I particularly remember a cocktail party that took place some years ago in the home of a very successful venture capitalist. I was invited because the host and my husband had done some real estate deals together.

The setting was elegant, but relaxed. In one corner of the living room a musician hired for the occasion played Beatles songs on a grand piano, while a sharply dressed young lady circulated with trays of hors d'oeuvres. I wandered into an interesting conversation with three venture capitalists (VCs). All fit the stereotype: trim, tanned, dressed in jeans and long-sleeve, collared shirts rolled up at the cuffs.

The conversation ranged from physical fitness to travel, and finally to investing. All three of the VCs had recently invested in a tiny new startup called Google. (No one mentioned Facebook, because at this time Mark Zuckerberg was just starting high school.)

After listening to these three men talk about how they used return-on-investment calculations when making decisions, I said, "That's what corporations should do internally. But in my job as a change management consultant at Hewlett-Packard, I see managers making a lot of bad decisions that are based more on gut feel than on data."

"Corporations already use ROI when making decisions about purchases of new equipment and that sort of thing," said Kevin, the host of the party. "What other kinds of decisions are you talking about?"

"For example, if they collected data on the performance of individual people in relation to the expected value of their roles, they could calculate the ROI of every hire," I suggested. "They'd have a better idea about what types of people to hire and how to make them more successful. They could also tailor training programs to the specific needs of each individual, instead of merely running everyone through courses chosen by gut instinct or according to the latest fad. If they had data on the performance of these individuals, they could measure the ROI of every training. This would be especially powerful for high-impact roles in sales."

"I'm all for making sales more of a highly structured, data-driven process, and less the domain of the 'wild west cowboy' types who excel in charisma, golf, and holding their liquor," said another of the men.

"But how are companies going to get this data?" someone asked. "What system would this data tap into to provide relevant information that could drive business decisions or be used to make predictions?"

None of us knew the answers to these questions. This was back in 2000, when the Internet was still in its infancy. The data may have been there locked deep in the data center on endless spools of recording media, but the technology simply didn't exist to bring this data to life and to support such futuristic thinking. The discussion tapered off and our group dispersed.

Later that evening, Kevin, one of the VCs I was speaking with, came over to me. "I want you to come to work for one of my startups. I think you can help them."

I'm so glad I accepted Kevin's job offer. It gave me the opportunity to put into practice some of the concepts we had discussed that evening. Looking back, I believe I was present at the birth of a vision for the transformation of the sales function. It's been my privilege to be part of the revolution ever since.

WHAT YOU CAN EXPECT FROM THIS BOOK

In these pages, I'll introduce you to PAM, the "Prescriptive Action Model" that my team and I developed. It is the first data analysis program that integrates sales, sales operations, sales training, marketing, IT, human resources, and other sales functions into a comprehensive system to dramatically improve sales effectiveness across an entire corporation. You will learn how PAM works and how you might adopt its concepts. And the information you gain will help you lead an initiative to transform your organization.

In addition to being informative and practical, I wanted this book to be accessible and enjoyable to read. So each chapter begins with a fictional story based on the lessons the contributors to this book and I have learned while working for more than a dozen companies (such as Borland, Hewlett-Packard, Interwise, KPMG, Microsoft, Motorola, Oracle, Salesforce.com, SAP, SuccessFactors, Sun Microsystems, T-Mobile, Verizon) over the years. Much of the story I tell may seem familiar, because the concepts, themes, issues, challenges, and characters are universal to all companies striving for excellence.

As you read the story, perhaps you will identify with some of the characters. You might especially empathize with the trials and triumphs of the protagonist, the newly hired chief sales officer of Trajectory Systems, Pam Sharp, as she seeks under intense pressure to turn around the sales function of her company. I want to make clear, however, that the characters and situations in this story are purely fictional. As the announcers used to say on those old radio dramas, any resemblance to actual persons living or dead is purely coincidental.

After the narrative section of each chapter, you'll find a commentary section in which I offer comments and practical suggestions about how you can harness the power of data analytics to revolutionize the sales management function and ultimately the success of your customers.

Although the approach described in these pages is applicable to customer service, product development, production, or virtually any other aspect of a business, I have two reasons for suggesting that you initially apply it to sales. First, about 80 percent of any company is typically involved with some aspect of sales. An initiative that focuses on sales will usually attract significant buy-in across the organization. Once you have implemented PAM, this dynamic new approach within the sales function, you can replicate it in other functional areas of your business.

Second, increases in sales performance are usually easier to measure than changes in other areas of a company, and the potential benefits of a change are greater. In manufacturing or engineering, for example, the major goals might be to increase productivity and reduce costs. Although these are very important, they typically offer smaller potential rewards than improvements to sales, and the results can be more difficult to quantify.

GOING HOLISTIC

Many companies have adopted bits and pieces of the approaches outlined in this book. But because these tools are so new, I know of no company to date that has fit them together into a comprehensive system that tracks and analyses customers, salespeople, products, and other data throughout the lifecycle of the sales process. But the proven value of data analytics makes this type of integration the logical next step. Creating a holistic, synergistic strategy and a systematic approach to data and sales is an idea whose time has come.

With this powerful concept, the whole is truly greater than the sum of the parts. There is no reason to wait to harness the power of data analytics. Smart companies will start the journey now, so they will be among the first in their industry to reach the peak and reap the benefits.

Speaking of peaks, I am a big fan of roller coasters. For me, one of the most exciting parts of the ride is the beginning. As my car lumbers up the first steep incline, I'm aware that awaiting me at the top is a tipping point. Once we go beyond that point, there is no turning back. We will pause there for a moment that seems like a minute. Then we will come hurtling down on our wild ride.

As a business leader involved with sales, you are about to experience that tipping point. Enjoy the ride.

IN THE BEGINNING ...

I was profoundly shaped by events early in my career that drove me to a deep feeling of responsibility for the success of employees in my company. Many years before it was acquired by Oracle in 2010, Sun Microsystems decided to shut down a manufacturing facility in the Bay Area and send the work offshore. Part of my job was to help the people whose jobs were being eliminated to transition through retraining into new employment outside the company.

Sun had known for years that they were going to close the site and let approximately 700 manufacturing personnel go. But management waited until just a few months before the closure date to start retraining. Consequently, only a handful of these employees found other work inside the company; the vast majority were laid off.

It wrenched my heart that Sun did not do more to retrain and retain these skilled and loyal employees. At a highly technical manufacturing site, if only these people had been given more time for retraining, they could have successfully worked as service technicians, call-center agents, entry-level engineers, and in many other jobs. From that point forward, I knew it was my calling to enable employees to gain the knowledge and talents they would need to meet and even surpass future performance expectations, so both they and their employers would become wildly successful. To borrow an expression from Wayne Gretzky, I wanted to help people "skate to where the puck was going."

I knew I had to start by mapping out my own future, so I chose sales as my area of focus. I naturally gravitated to sales, because in this field performance data is readily available and success or failure is plainly apparent. I'm a passionate, results-oriented, and competitive person, so the energy in sales is a great fit for my personality.

From that point on, I started gathering all the information I could about employee performance and about how I could build models to enable others to succeed. At most companies in the world, the learning and enablement function is antiquated. Even today, the majority of enablement departments report on attendance and Level 1 learner feedback, as if this makes a bit of difference. This is a sad situation, and I'm on a mission to turn it around.

The story of Trajectory Systems resulted from interviews with almost one hundred leaders who generously shared their insights and experiences with me. I am deeply grateful for their input. Their collective wisdom created PAM.

The journey that the sales leadership team traveled in this book is similar to the one that I and my contributing authors have taken in several different companies. It is my hope that the challenges they overcame and the successes they experienced while creating PAM will inspire you to embark on your own sales transformation journey.

## Chapter 1

PLAYING THE BLAME GAME

Pam Sharp, chief sales officer of Trajectory Systems, paced back and forth across the front of the conference room as the seven members of her leadership team filed in and seated themselves around the table. She found their jovial banter inappropriate under the circumstances. They obviously didn't appreciate the seriousness of the situation.

When Exalted Enterprises took a majority share of Trajectory Systems three years before, Trajectory's revenues were growing at the rate of 40 percent per year, and profits were climbing even faster. Although the company's annual sales were only $90 million, compared to Exalted's $2 billion, people at Trajectory joked about how the little fish was someday going to swallow the big fish. That was more than a year ago, before Trajectory's sales began to flatline. Now, even though it was only two weeks after the end of the fiscal year, word had somehow reached the "Street" that this once-brilliant investment had turned in yet another disappointing annual performance. As a result, Trajectory's shares had tumbled 8 percent in the past few days and showed signs of dropping further.

Sharp had been brought in to turn the situation around. Since coming aboard three months before as chief sales officer, she had spent most of her time racing around the world to help sales reps close critical year-end deals, dropping by the home office only often enough to get a pulse check on employee morale. Now she was about to shift her focus from putting out fires to building a sustainable sales function. Somehow she knew this first sales leadership team meeting of the new year was not going to be fun.

"We did some things right this past year," Sharp began, extending her five-foot, eleven-inch frame to its full height and making eye contact with each of her direct reports. "All of you and your people worked hard; sales of the new hospital system are off to a good start; and we hired twenty new sales reps who are now ramping up. Unfortunately, that's the only good news I have for you today."

On the other side of the large picture window that formed one wall of the conference room, the sun was shining brightly under a cloudless sky: another typical mid-January day in Palo Alto, California. The rolling green foothills that surrounded Trajectory's corporate headquarters on Page Mill Road projected a feeling of serenity, but serene was the last thing Pam Sharp felt today.

Sharp continued: "The bad news is that our sales fell 17 percent short of our goal for the year that just closed, and they're even 9 percent below the sales for the prior year. That's unacceptable. And to make matters worse, some of you forecast as late as November at the company luau that we were going to come within 5 percent of making our quota. Remember that? The Pina Coladas, the limbo contest, the fake sales projections. I don't like these kinds of surprises, and I'm sure you don't either."

An uncomfortable stillness fell over the room. Pam noticed that Cathie Martinez, head of sales enablement and training, was dejectedly hanging her head. Cathie's was a good but delicate soul, and Pam thought to herself: "I'd better keep an eye on her confidence, because we're headed for some even tougher times."

Sharp didn't have that concern about Joe Kirsch, however. If anything, her VP of North America sales was too self-confident for his own good. A former defensive back on the USC football team, Joe still kept his 225-pound body in game-day shape. More than once, Pam had heard him brag about how he had ended the career of a UCLA running back with a helmet-to-helmet tackle. Now she wondered whether Kirsch wanted to end her career in a similar fashion. He clearly resented being passed over for the CSO position she was hired to fill. While most of the other people at the table were attentive, Kirsch looked downright combative.

Sharp continued: "When I came on board, I promised David Craig that I'd fix sales, and I will." She didn't have to elaborate. It was well known that Craig, the CEO of Trajectory, did not tolerate missed commitments. "At the national kickoff for our reps, our theme for the year will be 'Go Big or Go Home!' Well, that also applies to each of us in this room. If we don't make our sales number this year, some of us, or maybe all of us, will be asked to go home."

Barbara Acres, director of presales, didn't appreciate Sharp's implied threat. On the notepad in front of her she sketched a rocket ship crashing back to earth. Underneath she wrote "Trajectory's trajectory." Yuri Vosnov, VP of product development, saw the drawing and grimaced.

Sharp went on: "Today I want to know from each of you your plans to fix this problem. But first, let's start with the numbers. Stacy, what can you tell us?"

Stacy Martin, director of sales operations, made her way to the front of the room. "Let's start with an overview," she said. She projected a slide onto the white board (see Figure 1.1).

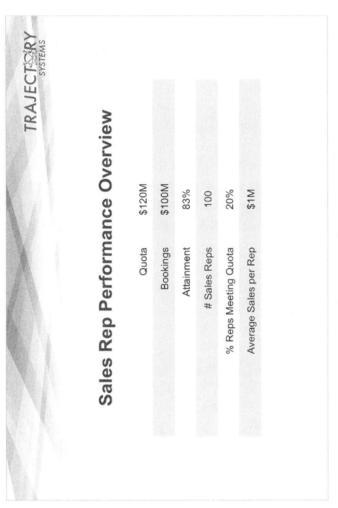

Figure 1.1 Sales Rep Performance Overview

"Like Pam said, you'll notice that we missed our bookings goal by $20 million, or about 17 percent. Out of our 100 reps, 20 percent made quota and half were below 50 percent attainment."

"That average bookings figure of $1 million per rep looks great!" said Raj Kapoor, director of marketing.

"Averages can be deceiving," said Stacy. "That average is high because a few reps did very well. Here's the booking distribution report (see Figure 1.2). As you can see, most of our reps averaged well below $1 million, and we had eighteen reps who didn't sell anything. I have a detailed leader board with names if you want to see it."

"You can't blame the reps for these results," said Joe. "They're doing the best they can with the products they've got."

Sharp, of course, had known about the large variations in productivity. In her three months of meetings and ride-alongs with various reps (she'd never imagined she'd ever spend so much time in various BMW 3-series vehicles), she had noted serious issues and heard lots of complaints about reps not receiving enough training or support. But she had rather expected these kinds of gripes from an underperforming sales unit during a major transition. Now, as she saw rep performances represented visually, she realized that the problems were deeper and more pervasive than she had imagined. Something had to be done, but what? The data didn't tell her what she really needed to know. She turned to Stacy: "Why did these reps miss their targets? Were they the wrong reps, or did they simply need more training? Was it a product issue, a territory issue, a pay incentive issue, or something else?"

"Probably a combination of all of those things," Stacy answered, shrugging her shoulders.

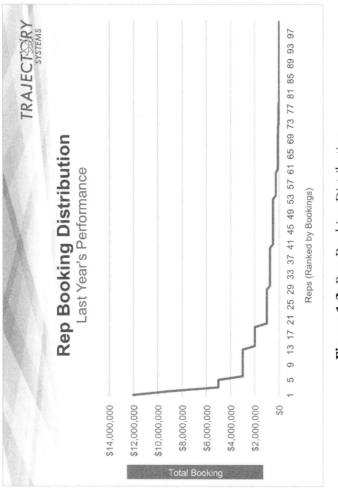

Figure 1.2 Rep Booking Distribution

"It looks like a few of our sales reps are playing a lot of golf," quipped Andy Mahoney, Trajectory's HR business partner. Most everyone sitting around the table snickered, except Joe. A two handicap, Joe's clenched jaw (which not surprisingly was as muscled as the rest of him) indicated that he had taken the comment as a personal affront.

"Most of those strike-outs were turned in by recently hired reps," explained Stacy. "It's taking us longer than expected to ramp them up." She put up the next slide (Figure 1.3). It showed an opportunity pipeline of $500 million, a win rate of 20 percent, and an average deal size of $100,000.

"That's more like it," said Cathie Martinez, the director of sales enablement. "An average deal size of $100,000 is terrific."

There was much less enthusiasm for Stacy's next three slides, however. The first showed no year-to-year growth in the average deal size; the second slide showed that the win rate for deals marked probable (that is, deals on the short list in the final stage of the sales process) was a dismal 30 percent; and the third slide revealed that the abandoned-deals rate was approximately 40 percent.

Sharp turned toward her VP of sales. "Joe, what do you make of these numbers? What's going on?"

"You can't blame me or my reps for missing quota," Joe countered. "My sales force is stretched too thin, and the new hires that came on board in the second half of last year aren't productive yet. On top of that, the economy stinks, our prices are too high, our products' technology is behind the competition, and our sales goals were too aggressive from the start. You know how they're set. David holds up his finger to see how the winds are blowing on Wall Street. Then he tells the

TRAJECTORY SYSTEMS

Pipeline Performance Overview

Total pipeline	$500,000,000
Average pipeline created per rep	$5,000,000
Win rate	20%
Total # deals closed	1,000
Average # deals closed per rep	10
Average deal size	$100,000
Total # Trajectory customers	500
Average value per customer	$200,000

Figure 1.3 Pipeline Performance Overview

capital markets what they want to hear and passes the quotas down to us. I had no say in our targets."

The fact was, Joe was right. And Pam knew it, but yet she still had a point to make.

"If the revenue goals were so unrealistic, why did you tell me in November that we'd come within 5 percent of making them?" countered Pam. "You had a full pipeline, and you projected which deals you would close. That didn't happen. Yes, you closed a few deals in December that weren't on your list, which is positive in one way. But it is also deeply concerning, because you didn't see those deals coming. Overthrowing the ball is almost as bad as under-throwing it. I have the impression that sales is operating in the dark."

"We need better leads, better advertising, and better support from presales," argued Joe. "Besides, there's only so much I can do with the current products. They don't have the features that our customers are asking for, and our demos are so weak they put our prospects to sleep. We're getting hammered by the competition."

"I can't give you better support unless I get more headcount or unless your reps do a better job of pre-qualifying leads," interjected Barbara Acres, director of presales. "They're constantly calling in and wasting my staff's time. Things will improve as the new reps get more training and experience, but for now, I'm doing the best I can."

"Your reps don't need more leads, Joe," said Raj Kapoor, director of marketing. "They don't even follow up on all the leads we give them. I know for a fact that lots of leads go entirely untouched!"

Yuri rarely spoke at meetings like this. So when he raised his hand to offer an opinion, everyone was surprised. Pam knew this was good and necessary if things were going to change.

"I want to get back to something that Joe said about our products," said Yuri Vosnov. "I can tell you for sure that our systems have features that our competitors' products don't have, and we're adding new features all the time. The product analysts rate us number one in our industry, so the problem is not with the products but with our sales reps. They need more sales skills."

"Hold on!" objected Cathie Martinez. "Enablement runs outstanding sales training programs. Class participation is up 40 percent this year, and the average participant feedback rating is 4.5 out of 5. I have a pile of emails from sales reps thanking me and saying how the courses have helped them."

"Yes, but the proof is in the results, Cathie," countered Pam, "and the results say their sales performance has not improved. Can you tell me which courses actually impacted sales results and by how much?"

"Sales performance depends on a lot of factors besides training," said Cathie. "It takes competitive products, good sales support, lots of sales leads, and so on. I can't give you data on the actual impact of specific courses, but I can assure you that we design our courses only after extensive interviews to determine the key needs that sales reps have. We're giving them the exact training they say they want. Like I've said before, you should make our core curriculum mandatory, so more reps would attend."

Sharp sensed the meeting was getting out of control. "All right, team," she said, in a tone of voice meant to calm emotions, "let's stop this blame game. Cathie, I can't give you a bigger budget unless you can demonstrate that your programs are having a positive impact. I need more than participant feedback reports." She turned to her VP of sales: "Joe, are you going to be able to make an 8 percent higher quota for this coming year?"

"I'm not making any promises, but I can tell you that if I don't get thirty more sales reps, we're *definitely* not going to make quota," said Joe, with a tone of finality that was clearly meant as a shot across the bow of this neophyte CSO. He was thinking that if the higher-ups had done the right thing and promoted him into the position of CSO, the sales team would be taking positive actions now instead of engaging in useless chatter.

"HR just hired twenty new reps for you in the past six months," said Pam. "Why do you need more?"

"A lot of the people they're sending me are not working out," complained Joe. "We've only had one star performer out of all the hires last year, and six of them left after only three months. HR is sourcing the wrong kind of people."

"Stop passing the buck," Andy snapped, "and don't blame attrition on us. That has everything to do with your leadership style and nothing to do with HR." Now it was getting personal. Joe had gone red in the face, and Pam was about to step in, but Andy regrouped. "Joe, just tell me what kind of people you want, and we'll source them. How am I supposed to know who works out and who doesn't, unless you tell me?"

"I want passionate and experienced hard-chargers who have great relationship-building skills and are strong closers," answered Joe with an insincere smile that looked more like a sneer. "Is that so hard?"

"It sounds like you're looking for clones of yourself," said Andy. Everyone in the meeting laughed. "Are you sure those are the kind of people you need across the board?"

The thought of more Joe Kirsches around the office caused Pam to cringe. One was more than enough. His attitude had soured so much when he didn't get the CSO job that many of his co-workers were beginning to lose respect for him. Actually, Pam was starting to think that Trajectory needed to transition to a different type of sales rep, or perhaps a variety of profiles to fit the different types of markets and buyers. But she didn't have time to think about that now. Out of the corner of her eye she caught Stacy Martin exchanging a "Get me out of here!" look with Raj Kapoor. This meeting was turning out to be even rougher than expected.

Throughout her life, Pam had always been successful. In high school she had been an all-state forward on the basketball team, president of her senior class, and a member of the national honor society. She had gone on to earn all-conference honors at Pepperdine University, while graduating cum laude. She'd succeeded in balancing a career and raising a family. During twenty successful years of increasing sales responsibilities and accomplishments in both big-tech companies and small start-ups, she had never failed at anything. She was a sought-after sales leader, known for driving turn-arounds in tough situations. But she had to admit that she was completely befuddled now.

Pam went over to one wall of the conference room, took a Dry Erase marker, and began drawing a schematic of the conversations she had heard in her short time at Trajectory, today's meeting being a typical example. When she had finished, she walked to the back of the room and gave the others time to take it in (see Figure 1.4). For a few moments there was absolute silence. People shifted uncomfortably in their seats.

THE BLAME GAME!

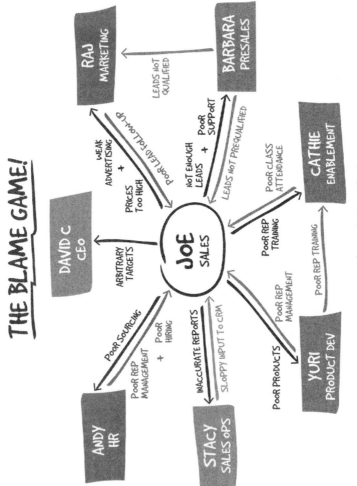

Figure 1.4 THE BLAME GAME!

"Pointing fingers and making excuses isn't going to get us anywhere," Sharp interjected firmly. "The only way we're going to turn this around is by working together. Now, I want to go around the table and hear what each of you thinks is the one thing we should do to get our sales numbers up to where they should be. Joe, let's start with you."

"I already told you," retorted the VP of North America sales. "I need thirty more sales reps. It's very simple. Take my quota and divide it by average quota achievement of my reps. That tells you how many I need. I also need more sales leads and more features on our products."

"That's three things," said Pam. "Okay, Barbara, what do you think we should do?" She shifted her gaze to the director of presales.

"If I had a bigger budget, I could hire more presales consultants and give Joe better service," said Barbara Acres. "Then I'm sure all the little Joes would make their quotas."

VP of product development Yuri Vosnov, seated to Barbara's left, spoke next. "We have a great product line, but we need to keep updating it. Some of our top development people defected to the competition last year, and we're understaffed. If I don't get more product developers so we can make a bigger dent in our feature backlog, our sales are going to suffer. I also recommend giving the reps better training on our competitor's products, so they can sell against them feature by feature."

"The leader board says it all," said Stacy Martin, director of sales operations. "We need to focus most of our attention on bringing the bottom-tier reps up so they achieve at least 50 percent of quota. I suspect they all could use more training, and we should probably let some of them go."

"Our top priority should be on improving our win rate," said Raj Kapoor, director of marketing. "And to do that, we need to do a better job of segmenting the market and creating specific messages tailored to each one. I can do that if you give me a bigger budget."

"The most important thing we need to do is improve our on-boarding process for new hires," said Cathie Martinez. "You saw all those goose eggs on Stacy's leader board. That's an indication of how much their slow ramp-up is costing us. What good will thirty new reps do Joe if they're still not productive after nine months? Any increase in budget should go to enablement. Training is the key to sales success, and it's the sales managers' responsibility to ensure reps attend the courses." Cathie glanced over at Joe, who seemed unfazed by her jab.

Everyone had spoken except HR business partner Andy Mahoney. "Andy, if you haven't noticed, there's a theme going on here. Do you guys need a bigger budget, too?" asked Pam.

"No. I feel everyone's missing the major issue," said Andy. "I think we should look at our sales management approach. We're getting a lot of negative comments in the exit interviews." As Andy continued on a diatribe that went on for several minutes, Pam's mind wandered … she wondered what she should do now. This had been a really discouraging meeting. Deep down she knew they were all passionate, talented people, but there's was no agreement. The only thing they agreed on was that their problems were outside of their control. Everyone had started out blaming each other, and they ended up blaming their budgets. She knew that throwing money at the problem was not the answer.

Finally, Pam thanked everyone for coming. She had to catch a flight to Dallas. "I'll have a draft plan when I get back. In the meantime, please document your recommendations and send them to me."

SUMMARY

Pam Sharp, the new chief sales officer of Trajectory Systems has been brought in to turn around the company's struggling sales organization. She convenes a meeting of her leadership team shortly after the close of the fiscal year to brainstorm about how to return the business to growth and profitability. Although her people are looking at data and reports, they interpret them differently and come to different conclusions about what actions to take. Their discussion devolves into a blame game where everyone is making excuses and asking for a bigger budget. Joe Kirsch, the VP of sales, says in a combative tone that he will never attain his sales quota unless he has more people. The leadership team fails to agree on a plan of action, and Pam leaves for Dallas, promising to present a plan when she returns.

COMMENTARY

Most of us would agree that Pam Sharp did many of the right things when she assumed her new leadership responsibilities at Trajectory Systems. She spent time in the field getting to know key customers; she sought to add value right away by helping her reps close some deals; and she asked for suggestions and feedback from her people. But none of it has worked.

The atmosphere at Trajectory is filled with confusion, blame-shifting, and excuse-making. The members of her leadership team are focusing on the problems and offering very few solutions. Like any other executive, Pam would love to hear: "This is the problem, and this is how I'm going to fix it." But all she's hearing is, "It's their fault, and I need more money."

Regardless of whether you find the meeting portrayed above extreme or all too familiar, you can probably identify with many of Trajectory's challenges. Sharp's people are all well-intentioned and intelligent, but they seem to be more interested in protecting their own turf than in looking at the big picture. From the security of their own silos, they blame their circumstances and each other for their problems. And without real insights into what's going wrong, that shouldn't surprise us.

Sure, they're looking at data, but they're viewing it from their narrow functional perspectives. This naturally leads them to prescribe fixes only within their own domains. But their issues with data go far beyond classic turf wars. The key problem, as we'll discover in the chapters that follow, is that they don't have the *right* data. They know they have problems, but they don't know why. What's more, they don't realize that the data they have isn't really helping them find the answers.

When quality data is lacking, it's difficult to arrive at useful insights about what drives sales. And without an understanding of what drives sales, it's hard to solve problems. We clearly see from the meeting portrayed above how inadequate data undermines focused action, which in turn almost inevitability leads to missed sales targets. The environment at Trajectory is characterized by dysfunctional behaviors, an absence of accountability and ownership, a silo mentality, an emphasis on efficiency instead of effectiveness, and a tendency to throw resources at problems. Pam Sharp's quandary is all too common among sales leaders today.

Sales leaders often bring in data about the *total addressable market* (or TAM) for their products, or sometimes they even have data about what sales competitors are earning in a given market. However, these approaches are rudimentary and lack sophisticated analytics. They may have worked in the past, but are inadequate for the operational needs of 21st Century businesses.

THE DANGERS OF MAKING DECISIONS WITHOUT THE RIGHT DATA, PART I: A PRIME SALES EXAMPLE

Pam and the other leaders at Trajectory Systems all want to correct their sales problem. But there's no agreement among the leaders, because they lack the relevant data they need to understand the issues, develop effective strategies, and make sound decisions.

Here's just one example—and a very familiar one—of what can happen when sales leaders operate without the right data. In our story, our VP of sales, Joe Kirsch, complains about the way the quotas for sales reps are set. His situation isn't unique. Many public companies follow the same procedure. After considering the expectations of Wall Street, leadership sets the corporate revenue target by dividing up the nut (revenue goal) and allocating it out to the various sales managers. The sales managers likewise allocate their goals to the supervisors below them. In the absence of sophisticated meaningful data, they usually make these distributions based on historical patterns and gut instinct.

Unrealistic sales targets can adversely affect the credibility and success of a company and the compensation, promotions, and morale of its employees. Unattainably high goals can create a pressurized environment that fosters anxiety instead of confidence. Not surprisingly, if targets are set too high, sales people may feel they're being set up for failure rather than enabled for success. We all know that the compensation structure for sales reps rewards success. People often say that sales reps are "coin operated," and for good reason; their compensation structure is highly weighted toward successful sales transactions. If sales people don't achieve traction fast, they will attrite and go where they can actually make some money.

In the past, many companies have gotten by with a haphazard approach to setting goals and rewarding performance, but that no longer needs to be the case. Indeed, it should not be. Today, companies can obtain the data they

need to set accurate goals that motivate and facilitate successful performance.

THE DANGERS OF MAKING DECISIONS WITHOUT THE RIGHT DATA, PART II: SOLVING THE WRONG PROBLEM

Worse than solving the right problem with the wrong data is
investing in the wrong problem altogether. Tristam Brown
is the chairman and CEO of LSA Global, a consulting and
training firm that helps high-growth companies perform at
their best by aligning their culture and talent with strategy.
Tristam follows the maxim that what can't be measured can't
be managed. (That's similar to one of my favorite expressions:
"If you can't measure it, you probably shouldn't be doing it.")
When talking with a prospective client, Tristam will always
ask, "What problem do you want to solve? What specific metrics will you use to gauge success?"

Tristam recently told me about a phone conversation he
had with the head of Sales who was interested in hiring his
firm. When he asked the prospect to describe his problem,
the answer came back rather brusquely, "Sales are bad. We
don't know why. That's why we need you to come in and
give a sales training program that will turn things around."

This prospect had no clue about what was causing his
poor sales. While on the phone with the HR leader, Tristam
did a quick Google search on his company. Within two minutes he found the latest analysts' reports, which stated that the
company was having problems in Latin America, and that their
cuts in R&D investment over the past two years had dimin-
ished the strength of their product offerings.

"According to your annual report, it looks as though you may not have a sales rep issue," he said to the HR leader on the phone. "Have you explored potential product and territory issues that may be negatively impacting sales? While we could certainly come in and put a customized sales training class in place and get fantastic learner feedback scores, we would not feel confident that we could help you increase sales with such an isolated approach. Based upon over 800 training measurement projects, we know that only one in five people change their behavior from training alone. While the percentage of behavior change will increase dramatically with the proper assessment, coaching, reinforcement, accountability, and support systems, sales training, by itself, probably will not overcome the more foundational product and territory challenges that you face."

The prospect got frustrated. "Do you want our business or not?" he snorted. "You were recommended to me and my job is on the line here. I need to put a training class in place, and I've heard that you're the best. Either you come in and teach my people some sales skills, or I'm going to go find somebody else who will."

Without a clear success metric that could be moved to make a positive difference for the client, LSA Global turned down this assignment. I told Tristam that I greatly respected him for making such an ethical decision. The client was not willing to dig deeply to probe for the real cause of poor sales. Unfortunately, this case is not unusual. Tristam told me that, in his experience, the vast majority of companies attempt to take corrective actions without understanding their root problems.

THE DANGERS OF MAKING DECISIONS WITHOUT THE RIGHT DATA, PART III: MEASURING EFFICIENCY WHEN WHAT YOU WANT IS EFFECTIVENESS

Many of the members of Pam's team are trying to justify their performance based on *departmental efficiency* instead of *sales effectiveness*. For example, Cathie Martinez, director of enablement, points to the feedback she's received from course participants. She has no idea how much her courses are impacting the effectiveness of her clients, the sales reps. HR business partner Andy Mahoney judges his performance on how efficiently he fills job requisitions. He has no idea how individual sales reps are performing after they're hired. And product development VP Yuri Vosnov measures the success of his department by how fast his people bring new product features to market, not by how eagerly customers are adopting them or how much value they are contributing to the bottom line.

When the various functional areas of a business focus on improving their own performance first and foremost, with little knowledge of or regard for how their actions promote the overall goal of sales performance, a silo mentality develops. As they fight for their "fair share" of the budget pie, employees in different departments become competitors instead of partners.

A corporation with a data analytics capability, on the other hand, can measure success by the much more valid metric of how well new hires actually perform over time. It can gauge the success of training by how much its programs impact the key drivers of sales, which in this book we refer to as *key sales variables* or *key performance indicators (KPIs)*.

Measures of *effectiveness* promote teamwork and cross-functional collaboration, because they align all functional areas with the same business goals. Discussions about priorities and allocation of resources become more objective and less divisive. Motivation and accountability increase, and excuse-making and blame-shifting decrease.

A key first step, then, is to understand what drives sales in your organization. Surprisingly, many leaders try to impact sales without understanding all the pieces of a sales ecosystem and how they interrelate. That's like a doctor trying to treat a patient without considering the anatomy of the human body. That's where we find our Trajectory sales team today—but not for long.

MANAGEMENT BY GUESSTIMATE

I have a confession to make. Over the more than twenty years that I've led enablement programs for companies, I suspect that some of what I've done has been a shameful waste of money. Sure, my initiatives to increase corporate sales effectiveness received favorable feedback, and no doubt they produced some benefits for individual employees, teams, and business units. But in the final analysis, most of the time I never *really* knew the financial return on investment from my efforts, because the data just wasn't available to answer that question.

This same kind of "management by guesstimate" is prevalent throughout every corporation today. Think about it. When a company's sales are trending below target, what's the typical reaction? Almost invariably it's to hire more sales people, conduct more training programs, expand into new territories, add new products, or take other actions that may have worked in the past. But these kinds of knee-jerk reactions can be a tremendous waste of time and money.

Today, thanks to plentiful data and smart analytics, companies can gain the insights they need to diagnose problems and make sound decisions. In my own field of sales enablement, for example, I know exactly how my programs are performing. I know which sales enablement programs to drive, because data gives me insights about the sales pipeline and sales skills deficiencies. I know who should attend my trainings, what trainings they should attend, and when. After the trainings are completed, data tells me in dollars and other pipeline metrics what effect they are having. I can plan my efforts for maximum impact and measure the results in terms of sales productivity. What a huge improvement from management by guesstimate.

That's why I wrote this book. I want to give you actionable insights into how to use data and analytics to drive measurable business impact that will positively transform your sales organization. In other words, I want to help you experience this same exciting journey.

Chapter 2

PULLING BACK THE CURTAIN

Sharp packed her laptop and work papers into her bag, exited Trajectory's headquarters, and waded into the sea of vehicles that filled the lot behind the building. She was so preoccupied with trying to unravel the conflicting input she had received from her team that for a moment she forgot where she had parked her own car, a yellow Porsche Cayman GTS she had recently purchased for herself as a hiring present. Every one of her leaders was fighting for a bigger slice of the budget. They were blaming others for poor performance, and no one was looking at the big picture, including her, she thought for the moment.

As Pam negotiated through row after row of cars, she was struck by the diversity. No two were alike. "People sure have different tastes," she thought. "Automobile companies that truly understand their buyers and know what they want have a huge advantage."

Suddenly, Pam was surprised to find herself standing in front of another Porsche: a red 918 Spyder. This was her absolute dream car, but the near $900,000 price tag put it far out of her reach. "I'd love to know who owns this," she thought, as she circled it admiringly. "This person must have been on the ground floor of a startup whose IPO really took off." She left her business card on the windshield with a note on the back that read, "Nice wheels! From another Porsche owner."

Pam had left early to avoid the rush-hour traffic, so she arrived at the San Francisco International Airport comfortably ahead of her 4:25 p.m. flight. She passed through security with no more than the usual delay, ducked into Peet's Coffee and picked up a cappuccino with an extra shot of espresso, and headed for the United Red Carpet Club, where she found a seat at a small table near a window. She had learned to rely on her creative intuition when confronted with thorny problems, so she pulled out a pen and notebook, took a sip of her cappuccino, and started thinking.

Determined to keep things simple, she asked herself, "What are the biggest factors that impact sales revenues?" Pam had thought about this a thousand times before, and she had always come back to the same fundamental sales formula:

total revenue = # of opportunities in the pipeline

× average deal size

× win rate

She drew a diagram in her notebook that showed these three variables under the general heading of "sales revenues."

"But every company is different," Pam thought, "and in order to impact these three key performance indicators, I need to understand what underlying variables influence them. Let's take deal size. It's largely a function of the number of products per deal. We need to drive up deal size by bundling." She wrote "# of products per deal" under average deal size on her diagram.

Across the room a woman couldn't get her toddler to stop crying. That set Pam to daydreaming happily about the days when her own kids were that age. She caught herself and pulled her attention back to the task at hand: "Now, what else impacts deal size? If we can go after bigger accounts, we can increase the number of units sold per product. Of course, a third variable impacting deal size is the price per unit, which is significantly influenced by how much we discount. This gives me a nice, neat formula:

Average deal size =   # of products per deal

× # of units per product

× average price per unit"

Pam added these key performance indicators to her diagram.

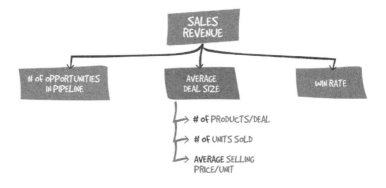

As Pam studied her chart, she realized that she had neglected to include another key variable: sales cycle. If Trajectory could reduce the time required to close sales, that would increase revenues. But she'd seen that strategy backfire in the past. Reps who were told to shorten their sales cycles often would begin focusing on smaller deals, so they could wrap them up more quickly. Besides, reps were notorious for not inputting data into the CRM at the right time, so she regarded sales cycle reports as too favorably biased to be reliable as benchmarks. She decided that for now she'd leave that off her chart.

An announcement that United Flight 6389 was boarding for Dallas jarred Pam out of her deep concentration. She collected her papers, tossed her empty cup in the trash, and headed for the gate. Once aboard her flight and settled into her seat, she realized how exhausted she was from the meeting with her leadership team. Minutes after takeoff she was asleep.

When the healthcare technology conference and expo opened the next morning, Pam stopped by Trajectory's exhibit and said a few encouraging words to the marketing team and the presales consultants who were staffing it. They were all bright eyed, confident, and eager. Since her role here was to be available for executive meetings if needed, she gave a key staffer her cell phone number with instructions to text her immediately if anything came up. With her sales challenge at the forefront of her mind, Pam was going to spend the rest of the morning seeing whether she could find any inspiration on how to tackle it.

As she made her way through the expo, she found a running theme: data and analytics. At one booth she learned about how a medical insurance company was using predictive analytics to forecast which customers were most likely to change plans, so they could offer them incentives to stick with their current plans. At another exhibit she learned how a government agency was using data analytics to predict which healthcare contractors were most likely to commit waste, fraud, or abuse, so they would know where to launch investigations. It seemed like everyone was talking about how they were using big data. "Maybe I need to get serious about this analytics stuff," she wondered.

It was dark when Pam exited the conference center and made her way to the taxi queue to head for Dallas/Fort Worth International Airport. As she stepped outside, a brisk wind and a cloudy sky reminded her why she liked living in California.

Back at the airport, on the other side of security, Pam made a beeline for the nearest coffee stand.

"Hey, 42!"

Pam instinctively turned because back at Pepperdine, she wore number 42 for four years. Sure enough, coming toward her with a big smile and an extended hand was her old basketball coach, Shep Wheeler. Even though he was well into his sixties, he looked as fit as ever. "Coach, what are you doing here?"

"I was recruiting a kid from a local Dallas high school," answered the coach. "Great to see you. Got a few minutes to catch up?"

During their forty-five-minute conversation over coffee, the two caught each other up on the events of the intervening years. It didn't take long for the conversation to turn to basketball. "You wouldn't recognize the basketball program now," said Wheeler. "We've gone completely into techno," he laughed. "We've even got a full-time statistician on our payroll."

"That's interesting." Pam said. "Doing what for you, exactly?"

"First, it helps us predict which kids are most likely to be successful in our program. It keeps me from wasting time recruiting the wrong prospects and it increases our signing percentage," he said. Pam was amused that she and her old school hoops coach had so much in common.

He continued. "I also use it in game preparation to predict what other teams will do. You know, what are their tendencies? Their patterns? It also lets me track what each player needs to work on to improve her game and which combinations of our players will be most effective during which game situations."

"Impressive," Pam said. "Mind if I call you sometime to talk more?" Wheeler gave his card to Pam as his flight was called and he headed toward his gate.

On the flight back to San Francisco that night, Pam's mind was overflowing with information she had collected about analytics. If she decided to install a data analytics capability, where should she start? Should she hire a consultant? Did she need to buy some expensive software? Did she need to spend eighteen months building a data warehouse? The learning curve was steep, and Pam was also leery of the hype that surrounded big data and predictive analytics. She had heard about some companies that had tried these things with mixed results. Maybe she should just get sales ops to give her more data.

Suddenly, the plane shook so violently that Pam felt compelled to grab the handles of her seat. A few seconds later, the captain calmly apologized over the PA system for the turbulence. He gave some specifics about the plane's altitude and speed, announced that due to weather conditions they were making a slight course correction, but that he was taking steps to make up the lost time so they would still arrive on schedule.

Right then, Pam decided she wanted Trajectory to be more like the pilot guiding the airplane. She wanted to know what he knew: where we are, what's up ahead, and what he needs to do to make sure we arrive safely and on time. "His instruments tell him everything he needs to know, so he can make course corrections as needed," thought Pam. "He's not up there saying, 'I wonder what will happen if I push this button or pull this lever' But unfortunately, that's exactly what I'm doing in my company. I'm not sure what levers to pull to drive sales. I don't have the data I need to make good decisions. I can see what happened in the past pretty well, but I have very little insight about what's coming up. To a large extent, I'm flying blind."

Pam pulled out her notebook and took another look at the chart she had begun developing yesterday on the way to Dallas. This approach of diagramming the relationships among the various drivers of sales had merit, she felt, but she had just scratched the surface. She settled back and began to concentrate. A short time later, her chart had several more entries.

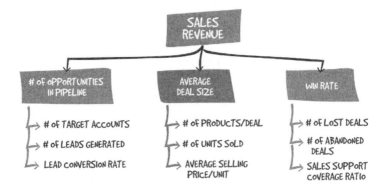

As Pam studied her diagram, she saw that she had the beginning of a classic key performance indicator (KPI)

map, a visual representation of the company's key sales variables. But something didn't seem quite right about the map's focus. Thinking back over her first three months at Trajectory and her conversations with various team members and colleagues, as well as the conversations she had had at the expo, she realized that the real key to increased sales revenues at Trajectory was improved rep performance.

"No matter how much Joe rants about hiring more sales reps, that's not the answer," she said to herself. "That's probably the most expensive route, and we already have too many sales people who are not meeting quota. Besides, it takes a long time for new hires to ramp up, so hiring is not the fastest way to turn things around. For now we need to forget about recruiting more people and concentrate on making the reps we already have more successful." She crossed out "Sales Revenue" at the top of her chart and replaced it with "Total Sales Rep Bookings."

When she got back to the office, Pam planned to have her team help her further break down the variables impacting each of the three major KPIs she had identified: *pipeline*, *average deal size*, and *win rate*. She was confident that once she and her team had logically laid out all of the variables impacting sales, the ideas would start to flow. She had a strong sense that data analytics could help her identify which sales drivers were most important and which were the weakest and most in need of attention and funds. She knew she needed a better understanding of what levers to pull to increase sales rep performance, but she had to admit that at this early stage she didn't know exactly how.

By the time her plane landed in San Francisco, Pam was feeling good. She didn't have all the answers, but she had decided to give data analytics a try: "If we keep doing the same old things, we'll keep getting the same old results. It's time for some significant changes. Our sales function needs a complete mindset transformation. It won't be easy, and we'll need some expert advice. At some point we may even need to bring in a data analytics consulting firm. But right now we don't even know what our problem is, and I don't want to outsource a mess."

SUMMARY

As Pam leaves Trajectory's offices and prepares to drive to the San Francisco airport to catch a flight to a healthcare conference in Dallas, she notices a $900,000 Porsche Spyder, her dream car, parked in the company lot. Curious about the owner, she leaves her business card on the windshield.

While waiting for her plane, Pam decides to take a structured approach to looking at Trajectory's problems by graphically charting the key drivers of the company's sales. Without realizing it, she is taking a first step toward data analytics. While at the conference, Pam discovers companies that are using big data and predictive analytics. Before she leaves Dallas, she happens to run into her former college basketball coach, who excitedly tells her how data analytics has transformed the way he recruits and coaches.

By the time Pam arrives home the next day, she has decided to give data analytics a try at Trajectory. She realizes that she'll probably need the expert help of a data analytics consulting firm at some point, but she doesn't want to outsource a mess, so she decides to begin by developing an internal analytics capability.

COMMENTARY

This chapter may best be summed up with this well-known saying: When the student is ready, the teacher will appear. Pam Sharp was ready for a revelation. Without sufficient data, she and her team had little ability to understand and solve the sales problems at Trajectory. Lack of data for solving problems is a common challenge that I often see when consulting with clients.

So Pam went back to basics and, as many smart executives do when they are temporarily stuck, began writing down what she knew. By drawing a KPI map, she gained additional clarity about how to tackle the company's problems in an analytical manner.

Conversations with users of data analytics at a healthcare conference and expo convinced her to give this new methodology a try. She also benefited from the input of her former basketball coach, who for a brief time played the role of a different kind of coach: her executive coach. His remarks sparked her interest in learning how data analytics could potentially be a game changer, literally.

If you aren't already seeing big data everywhere, it's likely you, too, will begin to notice it after reading this book. It's on the covers of mainstream newspapers and business magazines, and it's the subject of scrutiny in every conceivable trade journal. Now is the time to open your eyes to its potential for positive impact. This is not a fad; it's the new normal.

This chapter also covers a very "old" normal: the need to understand what drives your business. Whether you're in a global high-tech firm, a small-town manufacturing plant, a medium-sized professional services firm, or any other work situation, you need to be intimately familiar with what makes your business tick. You have to understand the mechanics of success and how to capture measurable results. Pam is wise to start this process and to involve her team in finishing it, as we'll see in the next chapter.

Pam's other major "Eureka!" moment comes when she realizes that her company's most critical driver of sales success is the performance of her sales reps. That may not seem like such a profound revelation. In every good company, the top leaders make statements about how their people are their greatest asset. But as Pam looked more intently at what drove Trajectory's sales, she realized in a more substantial way that the asset that drives all other assets is the innovative spirit of talented and dedicated people.

That's why she wisely decided to change her focus from improving "sales revenues" to improving "total sales *rep* bookings." Another reason is speed. She realized that she could almost certainly improve human capital effectiveness faster than she could launch new products, enter new markets, or make other major structural changes.

In our story, Trajectory's CSO experiences another key insight about human capital. Pam realizes, based partly on her career experience in sales, that throwing more reps at the problem is not the answer. At certain points in the lives of some young, fast-growing companies, hiring like crazy may make sense. But as businesses become more established and complex, leaders must be smarter about how to respond to challenges. They must step back and look more carefully at what levers to pull. Now that Trajectory is maturing past the "scrappy teenager" stage, it needs to adopt more systematic and intelligent decision-making techniques.

DATA ANALYTICS: GO BIG OR GO HOME

Thirty years ago, a company could be significantly behind its competitors and still stay in the game. No longer. Technology and innovation have accelerated the pace of change. Businesses that don't keep up will find themselves hopelessly behind.

Companies are scrambling to gain every possible competitive edge. For an enterprise-level company, even an extra 1 percent improvement in an area like sales rep performance or customer retention can add millions of dollars per year to the bottom line. It stands to reason that most large businesses can reap at least 1 percent of additional effectiveness by harnessing the power of their internal data already at their fingertips.

"The talk about Big Data is getting louder by the minute," says Josh Bersin, founder and principal of Bersin by Deloitte, a firm that delivers research-based people strategies to help leaders and their organizations deliver exceptional business performance. "As companies shift their core systems to the cloud, more and more people-related data becomes available. This, coupled with a tremendous focus on Big Data in the technology sector, has created a huge focus on data-driven decision making. The time is right for Big Data applications to explode in the next few years."[1]

Dr. Jim Gray of Microsoft Research believes that science is undergoing a "fourth paradigm" shift. The first three shifts were (1) experimental, (2) theoretical, and (3) computational. The current shift flows from an "exaflood of observational data." He maintains that with this flood comes both opportunity and the potential for expanded business.[2]

"The era of big data is upon us," declared *The Economist* in 2011.[3] According to Joe Hellerstein, a computer scientist at the University of California-Berkeley, we are living through "the industrial revolution of data."[4] Big data is a "game-changing asset," proclaims a 2011 report from the *Economist* Intelligence Unit.[5]

Given these clear statements that big data with its life-changing potential is here to stay, any substantial company that doesn't take advantage of its own geopbytes of available data is in danger of eventual extinction.

BEWARE OF THE HYPE

But of course, with opportunity comes risk. The shiny new toy that is big data is being hawked by myriad new players, not all of them knowledgeable or trustworthy.

At one outstanding conference where I was a presenter—the Sales 2.0 event organized by Gerhard Gschwandtner, CEO of Selling Power—some of the exhibiting firms purported to offer big data and predictive analytics services. But corporations in need of their help had to work hard to discern which ones could truly deliver the business impact they claimed.

A lot of vendors use the right terms: big data, data science, predictive analytics, CRM, data mining, business intelligence, machine learning, and so on. On closer examination, however, there's reason to be skeptical about how many of them are able to deliver on their promises. They remind me of the *Wizard of Oz*, but instead of hiding behind a big curtain, these "wizards" hide behind the marketing spin of big data.

Some of these vendor presentations actually make me angry. I listened to one supplier's pitch about how the data they analyzed and the programs they put in place resulted in increased revenues for one of their clients. But the presenter could not point to any evidence of causation, or even correlation, between the rollout of his firm's interventions and the client's increased revenues. The connection between the two was probably merely coincidental. Had his firm done nothing, the client's revenues might have increased just as much, or perhaps even more.

Many firms in the sales enablement space are making similar unsubstantiated claims. They offer no evidence of causality. Like the rooster who thinks his crowing makes the sun rise, they hype mere coincidence as correlation. It grinds me up to see firms twist their case studies to make them sound like peer-reviewed research reports.

"Hire our team of people! Buy our software solution! We'll provide the analytics services you need." Perhaps one or more vendors have already approached you with these claims, and now you need to make a decision. How do you gauge which vendors are reputable? Should you engage the services of a consultant, develop an internal analytics capability, or both? I'll offer some helpful guidance in the next chapter.

PULLING BACK THE CURTAIN

For many reasons, people who are not familiar with the world of data analysis can become frustrated trying to understand it. One reason is the lack of standardization in the field. The landscape is constantly changing, and the tools are rapidly evolving. There are many different but equally valid methodological approaches. Even the vocabulary is not standardized.

Because of these factors, you will find that no analytics taxonomy can anticipate every possible situation (including yours). Each dataset is unique, and every problem demands a tailored, creative solution. This book is not a how-to for data analysis. Rather, it is a guide to help you begin thinking in terms of data analytics and how you can use it to address your business challenges, which are also unique.

With this caveat, let's pull back the curtain and take some of the mystery out of this subject. Exactly what are big data, data mining, and data analytics?

Big data, also spelled Big Data (with initial caps), can have different meanings in different contexts. "The term itself is vague," says Jon Kleinberg, a computer scientist at Cornell University. "Big Data is a tagline for a process that has the potential to transform everything."[6] "In its most simple explanation, Big Data represents the ability to process a large amount of complex information to make better-informed decisions,"[7] writes *Forbes* contributor Sanjeeb Sardana.

Big data can also simply mean lots of ordinary data. "Most of this data already belongs to organizations, but it is sitting there unused," says Svetlana Sicular, a research director at Gartner, Inc., a leading information technology research and advisory company. Gartner refers to this hidden information as "dark data," because, similar to dark matter in physics, it cannot be seen directly, yet it is the bulk of the organizational universe.[8]

And we're talking about LOTS of data. According to Google's Chairman Eric Schmidt, five exabytes of data are created every two days. That is roughly the same amount as was created between the dawn of civilization and 2003.[9] We are now starting to measure the data universe in zettabytes. A zettabyte is 10^{21} (ten followed by twenty-one zeros)![10]

Data mining is the computerized analysis of large quantities of data using sophisticated analytical and statistical techniques to discover interesting patterns and useful insights. The information surfaced by data mining is often used in various forms of data analytics, which are discussed below.

Data analytics, also called data science or business analytics, is a scientific process for turning raw data into useable data. Jeffrey Stanton, professor and senior associate dean in the School of Information Studies at Syracuse University, refers to it as "an emerging area of work concerned with the collection, preparation, analysis, visualization, management, and preservation of large collections of information."[11]

THE FOUR TYPES OF ANALYTICS

As shown on the chart below,[12] data analytics is commonly categorized as descriptive, diagnostic, predictive, or prescriptive.

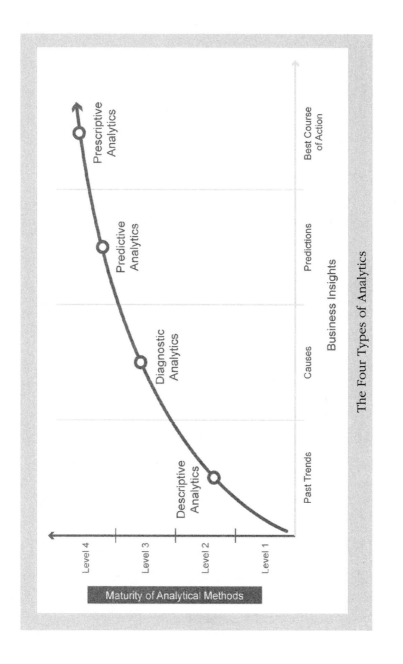

The Four Types of Analytics

1. **Descriptive analytics** asks the question, "What has happened?" It is the most common type of analytics used by organizations. By mining data to provide trending information on past or current events, it provides decision-making guidance for future actions, often in the form of key performance indicators. Descriptive analytics data is usually displayed within reports or dashboards, which are sometimes automated to issue alerts or trigger actions at various thresholds. In day-to-day business operations, a large portion of analytics is descriptive in nature. We will talk about these types of reports in Chapter 5.

2. **Diagnostic analytics** asks the question, "Why has this happened?" By utilizing statistical and analytical techniques to identify relationships in data sets and degrees of correlation between variables, it helps pinpoint the causes of problems and formulate corrective solutions. Trajectory Systems will begin to utilize this type of analytics in Chapter 6 of our story.

3. **Predictive analytics** asks the question, "What could happen?" The term encompasses a variety of techniques, such as statistics, modeling, machine learning, and data mining, which are used for finding correlations within big sets of current and historical facts, in order to make useful predictions about future events. Eric Siegel and Thomas Davenport, in their bestselling book *Predictive Analytics: The Power to Predict Who Will Click, Buy, Lie or Die*, define predictive analytics as "technology that learns

from experience (data) to predict the future behavior of individuals in order to drive better decisions." Trajectory Systems will begin to utilize this type of analytics in Chapter 7 of our story.

4. **Prescriptive analytics** asks the question, "What should we do?" It explores a set of possibilities and suggests optimal course(s) of action based on descriptive and predictive analyses of complex data. Utilizing advanced analytical and mathematical models, it can also provide reasons for its recommendations and possible implications of following them. We'll talk about this level of analytics in Chapter 8.

As you move through this book, you'll increasing learn about data analytics and how to apply it. Additional insights on the four levels of analytics are specifically presented in the commentary of Chapters 5, 6, 7, and 8 (one chapter for each level of analytics).

NOTES

1. "Big data in HR: Why it's here and what it means" by Josh Bersin; www.bersin.com/blog. November 17, 2012.
2. Markoff, John. (2009). "A deluge of data shapes a new era in computing."
3. *The Economist*. (2011). "Big data: Harnessing a game-changing asset."
4. *The Economist*. (2010). "Data, data everywhere."
5. Briody, Dan. (2011). "Big data: Harnessing a game-changing asset." *The Economist* Intelligence Unit.

6. Lohr, Steve. (2012). "How big data became so big."
7. Sardana, Sanjeev. (2013). "Big data: It's not a buzzword; It's a movement." *Forbes.* www.forbes.com/sites/sanjeevsardana/2013/11/20/big data
8. Sicular, Svetlana. (2013, March 27). www.Forbes.com.
9. *The Economist* Intelligence Unit. (2012). "Big data: Lessons from the leaders," p. 3.
10. One exabyte (EB) is equal to one billion gigabytes (GB). One zettabyte (ZB) is the equal to one billion terabytes (TB), or 1,000 EB. One TB is roughly the amount of memory in current-available for sale as portable consumer-grade hard drives.
11. Lohr, Steve. (2012). "How big data became so big."
12. Stanton, Jeffrey. (2013). *An Introduction to Data Science*, p. ii.

Chapter 3

CHANGING MINDSETS

Pam met with her leadership team on the day after she returned from Dallas. In the past, when the CSO went over a Trajectory procedural review, the solution had always been the same thing—more money. Joe Kirsch was especially buoyant. He figured that he had the new CSO over a barrel. If he didn't get the additional sales reps he needed, he'd simply threaten to leave and take all the good people with him.

"I had an interesting trip," Pam said to open the meeting. "I have some more clarity about what we should do." Seven faces looked up at her, eagerly awaiting the good news about their budget increases. Joe made a cash register noise: "Kerching!" Even Yuri laughed, and Pam forced a smile. "We're going to go in an entirely different direction." Puzzled expressions replaced the smiles.

"While I was away," Pam continued, "I attended some presentations that challenged my outlook. I talked to some interesting people, and I did a lot of thinking."

"I thought you were going to a healthcare conference, not a yoga retreat," Joe snorted. This time his joke fell flat.

Pam continued, "It's clear to me we're doing the best we can with the information we have, and we all know that's not good enough. But I think we can turn this around. In fact, I'm confident of it." Pam paused. All in the room were quiet and curious, the question on their lips: "How?"

"By improving our data capabilities," Pam said.

"Here we go again!" Joe said. "Another quick-fix fad. This had better be good."

Realizing that on some level Joe might actually be speaking for the group, Pam thoughtfully spent several minutes explaining data analytics and how it could be beneficial in forecasting sales, hiring better sales reps, measuring the results of training, refining the company's marketing strategy, and other aspects of sales. "I'm not talking simply about a new set of techniques," she said. "I'm talking about a whole new mindset. We need to really think differently about how we approach sales."

Pam added that she didn't have all the answers, that, in fact, she had more questions than answers, which is why she wanted to form a taskforce of four or five to explore how they might use data analytics. A few people had interested expressions, but others exchanged skeptical looks. Joe Kirsch looked resistant, even hostile.

"I've heard about this big data stuff before," said Joe, teetering back on two chair legs with his hands clasped behind his head so that his large presence dominated the room. "The government uses it to spy on people. Well, my customers aren't terrorists, and I'm not a machine. Give me my thirty new sales reps, and I'll do my job."

Andy Mahoney chimed in. Clearly this was out of his comfort zone. "HR should be about caring for people, not treating them as numbers. We might get some negative feedback from employees. Like Joe says, this big data stuff is getting a bad rap in the news."

"Geez, Andy, don't get soft on us," teased Raj.

"I'm responsible for *human* resources," replied Andy. "I'm concerned we could come across as Big Brother. If the whole thing backfires, it hurts morale and our reputation in the industry; then we can't hire good people and soon we're out of business."

Pam said that Andy was right. "We need to have a thoughtful policy that we share transparently with employees about what data we track, how we'll use it, and what decisions we'll make because of it. Our goal is not to spy on people, but to help them be more effective and successful."

"I'm willing to be on the taskforce," said Cathie Martinez, director of sales enablement. "Maybe if I had a way of measuring how much my training programs improve sales performance, I could more easily justify my budgets."

"You also want your training programs to be more effective in improving sales rep performance, don't you, Cathie?" asked Pam. "You're not just concerned about your budgets, right?"

"Yes, of course, that's what I meant," Cathie replied with a slightly flushed face. After years of focusing on training attendance and subjective feedback, this mind shift change was not going to be easy.

"I guess I have to get involved," said Stacy Martin, head of sales operations. "I'm the one with the numbers. I don't know how we can improve on the data we already have, but I admit that you've piqued my curiosity."

Raj Kapoor, the director of marketing, said to count him in. Yuri Vosnov, VP of product development, and Barbara Acres, director of presales, said they already had too much on their plates to tackle a new initiative, unless the CSO made it mandatory.

"That should be enough," said Pam. "We can start with a taskforce of Stacy, Cathie, Andy, and Raj. You people come to the conference room next to my office tomorrow at 2 p.m. for our kickoff meeting. Joe, I need a representative from the field. If you're not going to participate, give me somebody else."

Kirsch was leaning forward with his forearms spread out on the table in front of him. He twisted his neck and looked up out of the corners of his eyes to answer Pam. "You can have Jim Forrester, my western regional sales manager. He likes numbers so much he could almost be in sales ops. But you never answered my question. What about my thirty reps?"

"We're not adding any new reps at this time," answered Pam. "We will probably invest in more training to get some of your people up to speed, especially the new hires and our more significant under-performers. But I want to collect some data first to determine what kinds of training we need and who needs it. Trajectory doesn't just need a Band-Aid; it needs a transformation of the sales function, and this is the only direction that makes sense to me." Joe nodded and forced a smile. He knew he wasn't going to get his reps, and he also knew that some of his reps were "duds," as he called them to his inner circle. Pam thanked everyone for coming and they left.

After all had left, Pam felt deflated. Why did her leadership team have to be so divided and so resistant to change? Their silo mentality seemed to be getting worse. "This direction isn't easy for me, either," she acknowledged to herself. "There is no way I can lead this initiative without help."

Pam checked her phone and noticed that she had a text: "I got your card. Want to get together for some car talk?—Spyder Man." A break sounded like a good idea, so she texted back: "Lunch today? Meet outside cafe at 11:45. Brunette, tall, navy shirt."

A moment later she received another text: "See you there." Pam returned to her office, checked her email, and headed downstairs to the cafeteria.

"Hey, Pam! Wait up a minute." Pam turned to see HR business partner Andy Mahoney coming up to her. He spoke in a low voice: "I thought you should know that after the meeting Joe asked me to check the vesting schedule for his outstanding shares. He wanted me to calculate how much he would leave on the table if he quit now."

"Thanks for the heads up, Andy, but I'm sure he already knew the answer to that question, probably to the penny. He asked you because he knows that you will tell me, and he wants me to start worrying. By the way, why do you think so many of Joe's new hires are not working out?"

"Barbara Acres and I talked about this the other day," replied Andy. "From her position in presales, she has a good overview of the whole sales force. She talks about how customers today do a lot of online research before they even speak to a sales rep. When they do connect, right off the bat they start peppering the rep with questions about specific features, benefits, competitive differentiators, and other things. They want fast answers, not sales pitches. Barbara says that some of our more experienced reps who still want to sell by personality and discounts, rather than by opportunities and solutions, are having trouble adjusting. Joe is one of them."

Pam nodded. "That's what I suspected. Thanks." She looked quickly in both directions up and down the hall to ensure there was no one in earshot. "Say, can you discreetly gather some intel for me? I want to get an idea of which key sales leaders under Joe are so loyal to him that they might leave if he decides to go."

After thinking for a moment, Andy spoke softly: "Good people want to be part of a winning team. They want their hard work to bring success for themselves and their company, and they want to make the world a better place. They're loyal to leaders and organizations who inspire them and support them in achieving these goals. Keep focusing on making the reps more successful, and their loyalty to you and to Trajectory won't be an issue."

Pam smiled and gave Andy's hand a squeeze.

A few minutes later when Pam arrived at the entrance to the cafeteria, she looked around to see whether she could spot "Spyder Man." She didn't have any description to go on, but she figured that the owner of such a fine car would probably be a middle-aged, well-dressed, neatly groomed executive projecting an unmistakable air of success.

"Hi, I'm Henry Crawford."

Pam turned around. Standing in front of her was a guy who didn't look older than seventeen. He was wearing tortoise-shell-framed glasses and a faded yellow plaid shirt haphazardly tucked into his jeans and rolled at the sleeves past his elbows. In his hand was Pam's business card. "I own the Spyder," he said.

"It's a pleasure," Pam replied, shaking Henry's hand. "I'm Pam Sharp, and I own a Porsche Cayman GTS. But the Spyder is my dream car. They're so rare that I was curious who owned it."

As they went through the cafeteria line, Pam learned that Henry was helping a UC Berkeley professor build an analytics model to shorten response times at Trajectory's service center agents. They found a seat by a window and chatted for a few minutes about how the Spyder's 887 horsepower engine and two electric motors give it a top speed of 214 miles per hour and an acceleration from 0 to 60 mph in 2.6 seconds. Pam loved sports cars almost as much as sports, so she could have carried on this conversation for hours. But she didn't have hours to spare, so she asked the question that had been plaguing her ever since the two of them had met. "I don't mean to be rude," she said, "but do professors pay that well? How did you afford to buy that car?"

Henry laughed. "There's no money involved. I'm helping Professor Franklin just for some business experience. I got the money for the Spyder by betting on horse races at the Santa Anita racetrack. I developed a computer model that predicts winners with fairly good accuracy." He spoke these words matter-of-factly, as if it were the most natural thing in the world.

Pam became curious. "If this is too nosy, please say so," she finally asked, "but if you have that much money, why on earth are you hanging around Trajectory working for free?"

"I'm planning to start a business with a friend," Henry explained. "We're going to build a model that predicts customer buying behavior, hopefully sell it, and then move on to the next idea. While I'm waiting for my buddy to finish grad school, I thought I'd keep myself busy with Professor Franklin. It's fun and I need distractions to keep me away from the track."

As they continued to talk, Pam learned that this kid she mistook for a teenager was actually twenty-one years old and that he had an undergraduate degree in mathematics from Stanford University and graduate degrees in statistics and machine learning from Berkeley, where he had sat in on MBA classes for fun.

"Clearly you know a great deal about data analytics," said Pam. "I'm interested in how it might apply to sales. You know a bit about what we do here. What can you tell me that relates to our unique challenges?"

"Well, I can tell you about the horseracing model," said Henry. "A model for sales would probably be similar." The noon lunch rush had begun, and the din of hundreds of conversations now made hearing more difficult. Pam leaned in closer.

"For each horse I collect data on things like lineage, age, medical reports, training schedule, trainer stats, and owner stats," said Henry. "I also look at past performance, taking into account pole position, length of race, weather conditions, track conditions, time interval between races, the jockey and his record, et cetera. The model's predictions are sometimes wrong, of course, but all I have to do is beat the odds on average in order to make money in the long run."

Sharp realized that this conversation was similar to the one she had had with her old basketball coach. "Well," she said, "if you can predict which horses will win, can you also predict what kind of sales reps will be most successful and what types of customers are most likely to buy?"

"Depends on the data you have," replied Henry. "But from what I know about your business from my time here, I would say probably yes."

The two of them talked for a few more minutes, and Pam became convinced that Henry was just what they needed, so she decided to act: "We're under a lot of pressure to get some fast results. How would you like to help me with an important analytics project here at Trajectory? If your professor can spare you for a few weeks, I'd like to hire you on a temporary basis. What do you say?"

Henry nodded affirmatively. "Sure, sounds fun. But I'll only be here at Trajectory until my buddy finishes school. Then I'll need to focus on my own thing."

"Whatever works for you, Spyder Man. Can you start tomorrow? Our first project meeting is at 2 p.m. in the conference room next to my office." Henry said it was cool, but could they make it 2:30, as he wanted to stay for the first race at Bay Meadows to watch a horse run. Pam said no problem, and as he left she immediately group texted her team to say the 2 o'clock meeting had been pushed to 2:30.

SUMMARY

Back from the conference and expo in Dallas, Pam forms a taskforce to introduce data analytics at Trajectory. Some members of her sales leadership team are excited and eager to serve; others are cautious or skeptical, but willing to serve; and Joe Kirsch, the VP of sales, is so resistant that he has his western regional sales manager, Jim Forrester, serve in his place. Pam receives a text message from "Spyder Man," the owner of the Porsche Spyder, and they agree to meet for lunch in the company cafeteria for some car talk. It turns out that "Spyder Man" is an analytics whiz in his early twenties who recently finished college with advanced degrees in machine learning and statistics. He is at Trajectory helping his professor for some practical work experience before starting his own company, and he agrees to serve on the taskforce.

COMMENTARY

Because our story is didactic fiction, we're allowing Pam to launch a significant initiative right off the bat. But in real life, it's been my experience that huge initiatives that set out to change management perspectives and practices for an entire company frequently don't stick. Particularly with data analytics, it's better to think big but start small.

The results of data analytics projects can take some time to show up. While waiting for results, as the cost of the project continues to rise, management can sometimes get nervous, and there may be pressures to pull the plug on the whole initiative before the results are in. This danger is more acute when leaders launch a project hastily, without taking care to first socialize it among executives and gain buy-in from everyone involved.

It's often better to start a data analytics transformation by focusing on just one project or problem area. Use that pilot to test the concept, prove its value, and create a case study. Then build on that success and sell the concept to wider audiences within the corporation. Starting with a pilot also makes it easier to iterate, adjust, and refine the strategy and operational procedures.

If you start big and fail, you may find that people turn off to all future applications of data science. But when an initial modest project is successful, other people will get on board and your current and future initiatives will gain support. Over time, expand the scope and influence of your data analytics initiatives into other areas of the company. In most cases, cross-functional integration produces outstanding results.

LEADERSHIP IS KEY

Data analytics is most valuable when it is viewed not simply as a tool to solve problems, but as a mindset to increase overall effectiveness. This mindset needs to be translated into a solid plan supported by adequate resources, staffed by competent personnel, and led by a transformational leader.

"The adoption of a broad analytical approach to business requires changes in culture, process, behavior, and skills for multiple employees," Thomas Davenport and Jeanne Harris point out in their excellent book *Competing on Analytics: The New Science of Winning*.[1] "Such changes don't happen by accident: they must be led by senior executives with a passion for analytics and fact-based decision-making. Ideally, the primary advocate should be the CEO."

The leader of a data analytics initiative should have credibility, the ability to influence, and a reputation for success. In the case of Trajectory Systems, CSO Pam Sharp is capable of leading the data analytics effort because she has authority over all of the departments and functions that will be involved. As Davenport and Harris go on to say, "Any cross-functional or cross-department change, and certainly any enterprise-wide effort, clearly requires the support and attention of executives senior enough to direct and coordinate efforts of those separate units."[2]

The leader can be from sales, marketing, sales operations, learning, human resources, IT, or somewhere else in the company. When the initiative impacts the whole organization or a large percentage of it, the CEO, president, or COO may be the best overall leader or at least the executive sponsor. In some instances, the company might want to put a specially trained person or team in charge of the effort and bring in consultants who specialize in this field. Alternatively, create a special office for the leader that carries some sort of Six Sigma Black Belt type of status.

STARTING TO BUILD YOUR ANALYTICS CAPABILITY

Make the establishment of an in-house data analytics capability one of your long-term goals. Enterprise-level corporations without this capability will almost certainly be at a competitive disadvantage over the long term.

In 2011 researchers at MIT and The University of Pennsylvania conducted some of the first large-scale research on the direct connection between data-driven decision making and firm performance. Detailed survey data on business practices and IT investments of 179 large publicly traded companies found that those who adopt "data-driven decision making" (which they call DDD) have 5 to 6 percent higher output and productivity than would be expected given their other investments and information technology usage. They also found a relationship between DDD and other performance measures, such as asset utilization, return on equity, and market value.[3]

As you build up an in-house data analytics capability and adopt a data-driven decision-making approach, realize that it may not be easy to hire well-trained people to staff your initiative. The McKinsey Global Institute says that the United States alone faces a shortage of nearly 200,000 workers with deep analytical skills, and the shortage of managers and analysts who can analyze data and make decisions based on their findings is projected to be even greater (1.5 million).[4] This is what Josh Bersin has called the Talent Paradox: high unemployment that persists because unfilled jobs require skills that the unemployed don't have.[5]

FIRST STEPS

One of the first questions you'll need to answer when establishing a data analytics capability is whether to engage the services of consultants and, if so, when. In Chapter 2 of our story, Pam decided for the time being against hiring an outside consulting firm, because she didn't want "to outsource a mess." But she did recognize her need for expert help and, serendipitously, she ran into Henry Crawford.

In real life, you'll probably have to be more intentional about recruiting the help you need. If one or more people who already work for your company have strong skills and extensive experience with data analytics, you may be able to get a good start on your initiative without engaging outside consultants. As we tell you more of Pam's story, you will see that this approach has certain advantages.

On the other hand, you may find it best to hire a data scientist or engage the services of an outside consultant who can advise you from the beginning about how to structure your initiative. At some later point, you may want to bring in a data analytics consulting firm to help you execute your strategy. However, bringing in too much consulting power too fast can create confusion and rob your people of the opportunity to take ownership and grow. First, identify the skill gaps that you and your team have and bring in a point solution to solve specific problems, as opposed to turning over your problems to an entire organization.

Giving you detailed step-by-step instructions on how to build your data analytics capability is beyond the scope of this book, but here are some rules of thumb to start:

- **Don't rush to outsource.** You know your business better than any outsider. Start by developing key problem statements that will provide the parameters within which you will work. Then assemble a team, usually including some people outside of your direct staff, who will stimulate and amplify your thinking. Premature outsourcing can cause confusion and stifle organizational learning.

- **Software isn't a magic bullet.** Resist the urge to rush out and buy analytics software. Despite the claims of some software vendors, buying software will not automatically give you an analytics capability. Software will do you no good unless you have people who know how to use it.

  While I'm on the subject of software, I advise against hiring data analytics software salespeople as data science consultants. They are not in the best position to offer objective advice, and they generally don't have the depth and breadth of knowledge and experience you will need.

- **Do seek expertise (when the time is right).** Data analytics is a complicated, rapidly evolving field. If you don't already have in-house experts available, I am in favor of hiring a competent and reliable consultant soon after you have established your overall direction and assembled a few key members of your team. This expert should save you considerable time, trouble, and money over the long run by, at a minimum, helping you do the following:

  - Assess your analytics needs and develop a plan for building your internal analytics capability
  - Advise you about what software to buy (if any)
  - Staff your project

- Pick an initial project and set realistic goals for it
- Sell your ideas to various stakeholders and gain buy-in
- **Take care in selecting a consultant.** As I've mentioned, there are lots of vendors in the industry who dispense inaccurate information and promise more than they can deliver. Some tips:
  - Hire a data scientist who understands both business and technology. Find someone who will help solve your problems, not simply a statistician who will help you with the technical aspects of analytics. While a strong understanding of business is essential, experience in your specific industry usually is not important. As a matter of fact, you may be better served by a data scientist who has experience in a broad range of industries.
  - Request recommendations from trustworthy people who have successfully used data scientists.
  - Go to data analytics trade shows and talk to lots of people. When interviewing prospective consultants, ask how they have worked with other clients.
  - Regardless of where you may find a consultant, interview carefully and check references.

Most importantly, learn enough about data analytics to be able to ask the right questions. Even if you are not technically minded, you can gain considerable understanding by reading books and articles. After you have read this book, for example, you will have enough knowledge to fairly effectively separate reliable consultants from hucksters.

In bringing her team together to be a part of this change initiative, Pam demonstrated transparency and trust, essential building blocks to any transformational initiative. Embracing big data analytics can be an especially daunting challenge, even for those accustomed to change, ambiguity, and risk.

A key reason to proceed with caution, as HR business partner Andy Mahoney suggests in this chapter, relates to the potential privacy concerns around the use of employee data. Sales reps expect sales leadership to use CRM data to analyze performance, but when a company begins to bring together data sources from multiple internal systems to analyze performance gaps and propose solutions, employees may feel like they are in Orwell's *1984* and Big Brother is watching them. Even when the company's intentions are entirely noble and benevolent, employees will rebel if they feel manipulated or coerced.

Prior to introducing analytics initiatives to the company that may raise these concerns, leadership should discuss these ethical considerations and openly communicate their policies and commitments to employees in a manner that demonstrates awareness of these issues and respect for individual privacy. They should make it clear that the goal of the initiatives is to improve the success of individual employees and the company as a whole, not to punish or embarrass people who are doing poorly.

To be safe, the company should allow anyone to opt out who does not want to receive suggestions on how to be more successful and productive. Companies with international operations should check local laws. Some European counties have strict laws around the type of analysis that can be done with employee performance data, and many countries worldwide have laws about where that employee performance analysis can be done (that is, the data, the data center, and the analysis of the data must remain in the country).

Ultimately, employees want their efforts to be successful, and they want to be on a winning team. The great majority desire to perform to their highest potential, not simply coast along and collect a paycheck. Employees will readily embrace a data analytics initiative that helps them attain this goal, if it is communicated and administered with transparency and respect.

A successful data analytics program will help your people perform better, which in turn will make your company more successful. Success attracts success, and top performers attract top performers. It's a self-perpetuating upward spiral.

NOTES

1. Thomas H. Pamnport & Jeanne G. Harris. (2007). *Competing on Analytics: The New Science of Winning*. Boston: Harvard Business School Press, p. 30.
2. Ibid, p. 31.

3. Erik Brynjolfsson, Massachusetts Institute of Technology (MIT)–Sloan School of Management; National Bureau of Economic Research (NBER); Lorin M. Hitt, University of Pennsylvania–Operations & Information Management Department; Heekyung Hellen Kim, MIT–Sloan School of Management. (2011, April 22). http://papers.ssrn.com/sol3/papers.cfm?abstract_id=1819486

4. McKinsey Global Institute. (2011, May). Big Data: The Next Frontier for Innovation, Competition, and Productivity.

5. www.deloitte.com/view/en_US/us/Insights/Browse-by-Content-Type/deloitte-review/eadd148c49305310VgnVCM1000001a56f00 aRCRD.htm

Chapter 4

FINDING THE KEYS

When Pam Sharp walked into the conference room shortly after 2:30 p.m., Henry Crawford was already there chatting with Stacy Martin and Andy Mahoney. Raj Kapoor, Cathie Martinez, and Jim Forrester arrived a short time later. They were in a great mood, as Henry regaled them with the tale of his horse Tina's Dream winning by a nose and paying 13.20 on a two-dollar ticket. What he didn't tell them, but Pam knew having seen his Porsche, was that the kid probably didn't bet two bucks—more like 2,000. They all took seats around the oval table in the center of the room.

"I think most of you know Jim Forrester, our western regional sales manager," Pam began. "I need to say a few words about why I'm so glad to have him on this taskforce. Jim has been a rising star ever since David Craig recruited him. He started by earning Rookie of the Year honors, and last year he was our top sales rep in the U.S. He has a great reputation for developing the people under him, and he's very open to new ideas. Jim, Your perspective is going to be very important to us. We know you have a quota to make in your 'day job,' so my goal is to limit your time commitment to just a few hours a week."

"Thanks, Pam," said Jim. "It's my pleasure to serve on this taskforce. I hope I can be useful and learn something at the same time."

Pam looked in Henry's direction. His introduction was going to be a little delicate; she wasn't sure everyone in the room was going to be thrilled that she was going to rely so heavily on the Converse-wearing youngster. "Everybody, this is Henry Crawford. I invited him to be a member of this task-force because he's something of a whiz kid at statistics and

70

data analytics. He recently earned two graduate degrees in this field from UC Berkeley. And as a bonus for us, he sat in on MBA classes as a hobby. He's looking for a way to stay busy before he and a friend start their own data analytics company, and I persuaded him to help us out in the meantime."

Raj jokingly asked Henry how much he would charge to tutor his teenager to prep for the SATs. No one laughed.

Pam continued: "I know you are all very busy, but the work we will be doing is extremely important, so I need your whole-hearted participation. Stacy and Henry, I'd like you to consider this project to be your first priority for the duration. Now, I want to start by hearing from each of you about what you hope to get out of serving on this taskforce. Stacy, let's start with you."

Stacy was still processing what Pam had just said about the seriousness of the commitment, so there was a several-second delay before she spoke: "I'm curious about whether data analytics is different from what I'm already doing, and if so, how. I've thought more about what you said at our last meeting and I realize that the data I furnish is mostly about what has already happened. It's basically transaction reporting. I would love to be able to give people data that was future-oriented, so it would be more useful for making decisions."

Cathie Martinez, who was seated next to Stacy, spoke next: "Well, you're always telling me I need to give you data about the impact of my training programs before you will give me a bigger budget for sales enablement. I hope the outcome of this taskforce will help me be able to put that in more quantifiable terms. Plus, data and measurement are big topics in the learning field, so this is a good opportunity for me to get up to speed."

Andy Mahoney joined in. "I agree. If I can get better data on what types of sales reps are most likely to succeed, I can do a better job of hiring. New hires who are more capable might even be able to go through training faster, and perhaps they'd even need less training to get to full productivity. I think staffing and enablement can become great partners."

"I don't have any expectations," said Jim Forrester, who was seated next to Andy. "But the fact is, 80 percent of our sales team did not make quota last year. If what we're going to be doing will help with that problem, I'm all in."

"Joe's always complaining that the leads we pass on to him are no good," Raj said, "I'd like to know how we can do a better job of qualifying leads; that way marketing won't be blamed for the problems in sales."

Pam looked in Henry Crawford's direction. "Everyone's spoken except you, Henry. I take it you've filled in the gang about your success at the track; maybe you can tell us how this can contribute to this taskforce?"

Henry smiled at Pam. "My job is to help you think in terms of data," he answered. "With modern data analysis tools we can put together predictive models that have the potential to transform the way this company does business. Everything we need to start is already here. All we have to do is figure out how to assemble the pieces."

Pam got up from her seat at the table and walked over to the white board. "OK, our goal this year is to increase sales revenues by 30 percent. It's already been suggested that we hire more sales reps. We may end up doing that, but I'd like to put that idea in the parking lot for now. It's probably the most expensive approach, it would take several months for these new reps to ramp up, and a lot of the reps we already have aren't meeting quota. So it makes sense to me to try other things first. Instead of talking about hiring, I'd like this taskforce to concentrate on improving the performance of the reps already on board. I suspect that if we make a few improvements in rep performance, we will exceed our goal of increasing revenues by 30 percent."

Pam made eye contact with the members of the taskforce. Everyone seemed to be with her, so she continued: "In preparation for this meeting, I started making a KPI map for total sales rep bookings. As most of you know, the three components of the revenue formula are pipeline opportunities, average deal size, and win rate, so I began with those. Then I added a few KPIs under each of these areas. But this list isn't complete, so I'd like your help in fleshing it out." She sketched on the white board the KPI map she had developed while on her trip to Dallas.

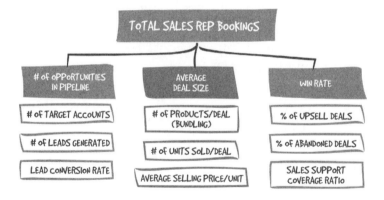

"If we can make meaningful gains in one or more of these three areas," Pam continued, "we should see a significant increase in rep sales bookings and quota attainment."

"I think we should brainstorm about how we can increase the number of opportunities in our pipeline by 30 percent," suggested Raj. "Even if we don't change anything else, a 30 percent increase in the pipeline will increase our overall sales revenue by 30 percent."

"That may turn out to be a good strategy, Raj," said Pam, "but let's first build the KPI map. We don't want to get into discussing solutions until we've collected and analyzed the data. The data may show that we would have greater leverage on revenues by emphasizing certain products, selling to certain markets, or making some other targeted changes. Trying to increase the size of the pipeline across the board may not be the best way to achieve our goal. Let's see what the data shows."

"I think I'm beginning to get it," said Raj. "If data analytics can help us focus on the areas of greatest impact, like maybe programs that would increase our win rate, we might be able to get higher revenues without actually generating more leads. That's a great idea. I always thought a pipeline of 4X wasn't very good, and out current win rate of 20 percent is downright pathetic. We should shoot for a win rate of at least 30 percent."

"I agree," added Jim. "We need to have a presence at more trade shows. That's where we do the best job of converting opportunities into deals."

Pam was ecstatic that the group seemed to be all moving in the same direction, but also realized that they needed focus. "I love what everyone is saying," Pam again interjected, "but we need to go about this in an organized way. At this stage we don't really know if a 20 percent win rate is good or bad. The data will tell us that. In fact, the data may tell us that focusing on the win rate isn't even the most effective way to increase revenues. Henry, do you have any suggestions about how we should proceed?"

"We're on the right track," said Henry. "The first step in any data effort is to figure out what data we need. The KPI map is a good start. We need to finish this step by filling out the map with any other relevant KPIs you can think of."

"OK. Step One is to determine what data we need by identifying the company's sales KPIs," said Pam. "Henry, why don't you come up here and put that on the white board."

Henry walked over to the white board and under the heading "Initial Steps" wrote "1) Identify KPIs."

"That first step is just what we're about to do," continued Pam. "While you're up here, Henry, let's look ahead a bit. What will come next?"

"Step Two is to find and collect the data behind the KPIs," Henry answered. He wrote "2) Locate and collect data" on the white board. "Data can be scattered in different parts of a company, and you have to hunt it down, so this step is usually difficult and even frustrating. We can expect to encounter problems such as poor quality data, systems not talking to each other, data getting lost, systems migrating, data simply not being entered in the first place, and so on."

Stacy nodded vigorously. "That's the truth! If I had a dollar for each of my data-related frustrations, I'd be a rich lady. But I volunteer to be the go-to person for data questions, so I won't complain when you come to me with problems."

"Once we have a clean data set, the next step is for me to sit down with the data and take a close look," continued Henry. "Each dataset has peculiarities, and in order to gain intuition, it's important to just spend some time plotting variables against each other and looking at things like averages of each variable."

"Sorry to interrupt," said Pam, "but can you explain what you mean by plotting variables against each other?"

Henry paused for a moment before answering: "Thanks for stopping me. I can be forgetful about using tech-speak without first defining it. 'Variable' is just another way to say KPI. So by plotting variables against each other, I mean making lots of charts that help me visually understand how different KPIs interact. For example, one chart might be 'number of sales versus tenure at the company,' while another might be 'tenure at the company versus attainment percentage.' With this kind of basic but important analysis, we can identify patterns, trends, and problem areas. In data analytics parlance, this is called descriptive analytics." Henry added that to the list on the white board, so it now read as follows:

INITIAL STEPS

1) IDENTIFY KPIS

2) LOCATE AND COLLECT DATA

3) ANALYZE DATA AND
IDENTIFY ISSUES
(DESCRIPTIVE ANALYTICS)

"That's probably as far ahead as we need to look right now," said Pam. "Henry, I'd like you to continue to be our scribe. Let's start brainstorming KPIs, which, as Henry said, we can also call variables. Who would like to begin?"

Andy piped up: "Hold on! I think we're forgetting a fourth area, something very key to rep attainment: motivation. This isn't touchy-feely HR-speak. There's plenty of research that shows that when sales reps are motivated and engaged, their morale goes up, and that causes their performance to improve. And we all know that the right compensation is big motivation for sales reps. We can't ignore these factors."

"I can't argue with that," said Pam. "What do you think about including rep motivation or engagement as a KPI that influences sales performance, Henry?"

"Throw it in. Better to have too many KPIs than too few. But please keep this in mind: we need to be able to look at variables that are quantifiable on an individual level, and we may not be able to do that with HR data because of privacy concerns."

"Oh, you're right! I should have put that together." said Andy, laughing at his mistake. "Henry makes a good point. The only way we can quantify motivation is through employee engagement survey scores, and we can only look at those in aggregate and by department, not by individual rep."

Pam liked to see this type of critical thinking: "I like where you're going with this, Andy. We could track how much engagement scores improve for all reps, but for now we should probably just look at motivation separately, not as part of our KPI map. But what about other HR data, like tenure, experience, and so on? Seems like those would be very relevant, and we can definitely find that information."

"Sure, sounds good," said Henry.

"I'll start gathering all the HR data I have that is at the individual rep level," said Andy, starting a list for himself in his notebook.

"Let's move forward with identifying some more KPIs," said Pam. "Where do we begin?"

"I suggest we start with deal size," said Jim. "That's always been a struggle with my team."

"OK, let's start there." said Pam, pleased to see that he was on her wavelength. "Jim, start us off, what do you see as the key drivers that impact deal size?"

"One major factor is how much bundling our reps are doing," said Jim. "And that largely depends on their knowledge of our overall product line, especially about which products most naturally sell together. If they don't have this knowledge, they'll just push the products they're most familiar with. We need to make sure each rep has a nice, big individual product pipeline."

"Sounds good, Jim," said Pam. "Henry, how do you think we should express those factors as KPIs on our map?"

"Here's what I'd suggest," said Henry. He wrote on the KPI map, underneath average deal size, "# of unique products in the pipeline per rep" and "% of bundled product deals."

"We're off to a great start!" said Pam. "What's next?"

"For number of units sold per product, I'm always looking at how we can increase our focus on larger accounts," said Stacy. "That will definitely grow our pipeline."

"So how should we express that as a KPI?" asked Henry.

"Maybe we should track what percentage of our pipeline opportunities are with large accounts," said Stacy. "And we could also track how many of our deals are multi-year contracts. My sense is that our reps are selling too many single-year contracts. And yes, Henry, I know you want to see these expressed as KPIs, so how about 'percentage of large accounts' and 'average contract length'?"

"That brings up another point," said Henry, as he added these KPIs to the map. "We're going to need to be very precise with our definitions. For example, what is a 'large account'? We'll have to define that carefully and stick to our definition."

"Can you two work offline to come up with these definitions for later discussion and review by the taskforce?" asked Pam. Stacy and Jim nodded affirmatively as they made notes in their notebooks.

"OK, fantastic! We're on a roll," said Pam. "How about price per unit?"

"Well, we could certainly stop discounting so much," said Stacy. "I know the sales reps love their discounts, but sometimes I think we lean on price breaks too often. We actually ran some numbers recently and found that the average selling price is higher for deals that we win. So price may not be as big a factor as we think."

"Wait a minute, Stacy!" cried Jim. "Don't mess with our discounts."

"Sorry, Jim, but we've got to hit that 30 percent target somehow," said Pam. "And while we're on the subject of reps, it would be great if they could focus on high-value products, so these products would make up a bigger percentage of our overall pipeline. That would certainly drive revenue up."

"OK, two more KPIs," said Henry. He wrote "average discount rate" and "% of pipeline focused on high value products" on the KPI map.

"This is a great start," commented Pam. "Let's shift our focus to another area. How about developing some KPIs for win rate?"

Throughout the afternoon, the team continued to brainstorm. By late afternoon their map contained approximately thirty KPIs.

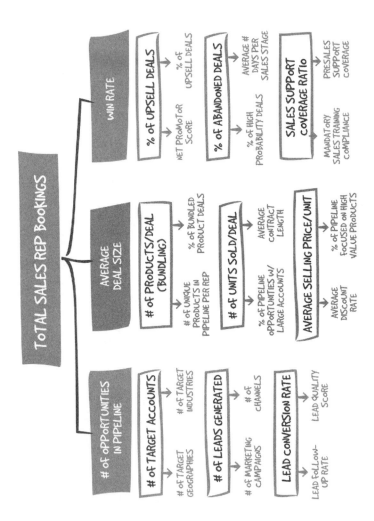

TOTAL SALES REP BOOKINGS

WIN RATE
- % of UPSELL DEALS
  - NET PROMOTER SCORE
  - % of UPSELL DEALS
- % of ABANDONED DEALS
  - % of HIGH PROBABILITY DEALS
  - AVERAGE # DAYS PER SALES STAGE
- SALES SUPPORT COVERAGE RATIO
  - MANDATORY SALES TRAINING COMPLIANCE
  - PRESALES SUPPORT COVERAGE

AVERAGE DEAL SIZE
- # of PRODUCTS/DEAL (BUNDLING)
  - # of UNIQUE PRODUCTS IN PIPELINE PER REP
  - % of BUNDLED PRODUCT DEALS
- # of UNITS SOLD/DEAL
  - % of PIPELINE OPPORTUNITIES W/ LARGE ACCOUNTS
  - AVERAGE CONTRACT LENGTH
- AVERAGE SELLING PRICE/UNIT
  - AVERAGE DISCOUNT RATE
  - % of PIPELINE FOCUSED ON HIGH VALUE PRODUCTS

# of OPPORTUNITIES IN PIPELINE
- # of TARGET ACCOUNTS
  - # of TARGET GEOGRAPHIES
  - # of TARGET INDUSTRIES
- # of LEADS GENERATED
  - # of MARKETING CAMPAIGNS
  - # of CHANNELS
- LEAD CONVERSION RATE
  - LEAD FOLLOW-UP RATE
  - LEAD QUALITY SCORE

As they paused to admire their work, Jim spoke: "At the last company I worked for, some consultants came in and did a map that looked sort of like that. But they used something called a Balanced Scorecard process, and the structure they came up with was different from ours. What's the difference between that approach and what we're doing?"

"Balanced Scorecard is a popular framework used to arrive at KPIs, KPI targets, and initiatives to drive KPI performance," said Henry. "We might want to use it in the future. But what we're doing here should work fine as well. The important thing is to identify all the possible variables that impact our desired outcome, which is to have our sales reps hit that target of a 30 percent increase in revenues. We've done a really good job of that, and now we need to talk about where to find and collect the data on all of these KPIs."

Pam turned to her director of sales operations. "Stacy, can we get the data for these KPIs?"

"Well, we can get the data, but it won't be simple," said Stacy. "But I did some of this type of thing at previous companies, and we can follow the same basic process. First, as we already did, we have to identify all of the KPIs that we need. In our case there will be dozens of these variables." She gestured at the white board.

"The first step is to agree on and write down the formula for each KPI," continued Stacy. "For example, average deal size per rep is calculated by dividing the total value of opportunities by the total count of opportunities per rep."

"What do you mean by 'opportunities'?" said Raj.

"We have to decide that," Stacy answered. "It could be only the opportunities that have been won and closed, all opportunities in the pipe, or maybe something else."

"The important thing is for our definitions to be clear and consistent, or the whole data analytics exercise will give us poor results," said Henry.

"It sounds like this step will take some time," said Pam. "Stacy, you and Henry find a quiet spot somewhere tomorrow and hammer out these values. If you have trouble with any of them, bring your questions back to the taskforce and we'll make a joint decision."

Stacy paused for a moment to see whether there were any questions before proceeding: "The second step is to identify the list of data elements we need and map out which databases house them. A lot of our data here at Trajectory will come from the CRM, but some will come from the customer database, the HRIS, and the LMS. And I wouldn't be surprised if some of it came from spreadsheets on different people's computers. That happened a lot at my last company."

"I'm familiar with CRM, but what in the world are HRIS and LMS?" asked Henry.

"Sorry, Henry," said Stacy. "I forget they don't cover that in college. HRIS stands for human resources information system, and LMS is an acronym for learning management system."

"Got it," said Henry.

"The third step is to figure out who can give us access to these databases," continued Stacy. "But you should be aware that our data quality isn't great. We have huge issues because system users and administrators don't always enter data correctly."

"That sounds good. Once we have access to the data, we'll have to pull it, and then we'll have to clean it up so it's usable," said Henry. "Cleaning data is my least favorite part of doing data work, but it has to be done. Missing data can really mess up a carefully tuned model, so you have to remove it. Sometimes the data isn't missing, but only incorrectly entered, and that can cause havoc, too. There are other potential issues, but I don't want to get lost in the weeds here." Henry turned to the board and added these and the steps Stacy had mentioned to the list of initial steps on the white board.

INITIAL STEPS

1) IDENTIFY KPIS
2) LOCATE AND COLLECT DATA
   - IDENTIFY SOURCES (DATABASES) OF KPIS (VARIABLES)
   - GAIN ACCESS TO DATABASES
   - PULL DATA
   - CLEAN DATA
3) ANALYZE DATA AND IDENTIFY ISSUES (DESCRIPTIVE ANALYTICS)

"OK, folks, it's getting late," said Pam. "Let's call it a day and finish this KPI map tomorrow. When we're done, I expect that it will contain at least twice this many KPIs."

"I vote that we keep going while we have the momentum," said Raj. "If we order pizza and have it delivered, we can finish this tonight."

"I've got a better idea," said Pam. "Henry and I will pick up the pizza. Henry, you drive!"

It was after 11:00 p.m. when the intrepid crew finished fleshing out the KPI map. The white board now contained more than one hundred variables that could impact sales performance, including macro-economic factors, market share of competitors, win/loss rate by competitor, and HR factors, such as average tenure of the sales team and team size per manager.

"Dealing with all of these variables is going be a daunting task," said Stacy, taking a photo of the white board with her cell phone. "The data we need for some of them is either too complex to easily retrieve or too corrupt to use."

"Good point, Stacy," said Pam. "When you and Henry are defining the values for the KPIs, make a list of which KPIs you think we should remove from our map. OK, I think that's enough for tonight. You've all done great work."

On the way out of the conference room, Henry turned to Stacy: "Can I have access to the data you based your reports on? I might be able to use it to uncover some initial insights on some of the KPIs we just mapped out. It might sound crazy, but if you can get me access before you head home, I'll keep working. I like staying up when I'm in the zone."

SUMMARY

Pam kicks off the first taskforce meeting, and the members share what they hope to contribute and learn from their involvement. The taskforce builds a key performance indicator (KPI) map, which identifies where they need to focus their efforts in order to improve sales rep performance. They also discuss how to locate the sources of the data they need, gain access to it, appropriate it, and clean it in preparation for analytical processing. This KPI map will lay the groundwork for descriptive analytics, which will help the team better understand the issues they need to address as they seek to chart a course forward.

COMMENTARY

The first step of any analysis is determining what to analyze. In this chapter, the analytics taskforce sets out to identify the key factors that influence Trajectory's sales. Once they have identified these sales drivers, which they also refer to as key performance indicators (KPIs) or variables, they can analyze data related to them and use the insights they gain to formulate strategies for improvement.

The taskforce is finding it helpful to portray these key performance indicators in the form of a KPI map. This graphical representation enables them to better understand how the different variables interact with each other, and it helps them clarify the types of data they want to collect and analyze. These KPIs are hypothetical influencers. The team members are making assumptions about what they are and how they affect sales. They will learn more about their actual impact after they collect and analyze the data.

Jim Forrester notes in our story that Trajectory's KPIs are different from those of other companies he has worked for. That's to be expected. Drivers of sales vary from company to company, depending on the type of industry and other factors. Your company's KPIs will be unique, too.

Our taskforce is using an informal brainstorming process to build Trajectory's KPI map. A consultant who specializes in the field of data analytics might have used a more formal approach, such as the Balanced Scorecard methodology. This is a procedure for adding strategic non-financial performance measures to traditional financial metrics, so that, according to the Balanced Scorecard Institute,[1] managers and executives will have "a 'balanced' view of organizational performance for planning strategic actions on a daily basis."

When implementing changes of this magnitude, it's fine to be informal, as long as informality doesn't degenerate into unprofessionalism. Notice how Pam skillfully guides the discussion. She avoids being confrontational, listens to all comments, and accepts all input without being judgmental. This encourages her team to express and entertain innovative and creative ideas. Because of her positive leadership, the participants do not engage in blaming, criticizing, or excuse-making. Those negative behaviors discourage collaboration and break-through thinking. The team instead starts to ask great questions and build the needed momentum to see this data initiative through.

AFTER THE WHAT, THE WHERE: THE CHALLENGES OF DATA SOURCES

After you've identified your organization's KPIs for sales, the next step is to determine the sources of data for those KPIs. In our story, the taskforce spent considerable time talking about what data to collect and how to collect it. Data collection can be quite a challenge. Here are some good rules to guide you:

- **Cast a wide net.** Data will not simply come from one source, so you need to look both inside and outside the company. If you define your data source too narrowly, your analysis will fail to produce meaningful insights. As a matter of fact, it may produce erroneous results that could lead to costly mistakes.

- **Consider exclusions.** You need to be aware of not only what you are including in your data samples, but what you are excluding. For example, we've only been talking about rep performance. We haven't been talking about customer retention, because that pertains to the *draining* of revenue rather than *gaining* of revenue. We haven't focused on attrition or sales profit margins either, because many companies don't measure their reps' performance based on these parameters.

  But if in your company you have responsibility for customer retention and/or profit margins, make sure you include those areas in your KPI map and in your subsequent analyses. There is no cookie-cutter approach.

Follow the steps outlined above and find the KPIs that are relevant to your situation.

- **Be sensitive to sensitivities (and politics).** Collect the data you need in an organized and thoughtful way. People are naturally hesitant to release data for analysis, because they're nervous about what it might reveal about their own performance. They don't want to be seen as part of the problem. When collecting data, you must develop trust and explain how you will use it. Without such trust, data collection can create suspicions, stimulate a silo mentality, and ferment political conflict.

- **Marshall the right human resources.** Your company may have a database in each business unit and a database administrator to go with it. Or, if you're lucky, you may have one centralized data store and a single point of contact. In either case, you and your data analyst will have to meet with the database administrators and their managers, describe your project, and work together to find the data you need.

- **Communicate your needs.** It's important to be very clear and precise about your data needs up-front. Your data team will need to provide a full list of the KPIs you require, specify the preferred format for the data (comma-separated values, or CSV files, is a popular format), and ask what is available for easy access. You may be able to immediately get some data fields, while other fields may require more technical wizardry or additional permissions from stakeholders.

- **Be patient.** Change takes time and requires the faith and cooperation of mere mortals. This is more true for data analytics than for many other endeavors.

THE EMPLOYEE LIFE CYCLE

Another helpful way to determine your data sources for sales reps is to take a holistic look at the employee life cycle. As depicted on the chart below (see Figure 4C.1), improvement in rep performance can be influenced in many ways within at least five different stages. To have the most productive reps, you want to hire the right candidates, train them well, enable them with the right tools and information, manage them effectively, and open up opportunities for them to grow or exit. Analytics can give you the ability to make the correct performance-enhancing decisions at all of these points.

BUT WAIT, THERE'S MORE: CARE AND FEEDING FOR YOUR DATA

There are two more key steps before you can begin to get serious about the analytics at hand: (1) assembling the KPIs and (2) cleaning the data. To assemble the KPIs, your data team will have to find out what data "fields" are available in the databases and how to combine them. For example, if your KPI of interest is "selling price per unit," you will have to pull the fields "total selling price" and "number of units" for every deal, and divide the former by the latter. KPIs can vary in how many fields are required to create them.

Recruiting	Training	Enabling	Managing	Growing/Exiting
Years of prior sales exp	Training compliance	% of deals via lead gen	Remove office/ onsite office	Promotions
Years in information sales	Trainings taken	% of deals referred by ISR	3 years attainment	Segment transfer
Prior job roles	Accreditation completed	% of pipe with partner	Opportunities created/ mo	Y-o-Y quota increase
Segment experience	Training scores	CRM usage frequency	Average deal size	Y-o-Y average booking
Education		CRM data field coverage	Median deal size	Improvement in performance stack
Performance history		Top lead sources used	Average product per deal	Last 2 quarters of voluntary attrition pool
Recruitment channel		Competition	Product coverage	Last 2 quarters performance of involuntary attrition pool
Tenure in the org		Usage of sales enablement resources	Roll over pipe	
Promotions/ Transfers		Pre-sales request	Conversion ratio	
Hired by manager, etc.		RFPs support	Quarterly performance trend	
			Sales cycle	
			Revenue generated/ mo	
			% of new business	
			% of license vs service rev	

Figure 4C.1 Data Sources Across the Employee Life Cycle

Some are straightforward, while others may need convoluted algebra to combine five fields into a single KPI.

Once the data from a variety of sources is in hand, it will have to be merged into a single data set. This can be tricky and is best left to data professionals. The freshly merged data set will then have to be cleaned; this is another process best left to experienced staff. Improperly handled data can lead to erroneous conclusions and misplaced confidence, leading to faulty actions. In short, it can do more harm than good. Don't skimp on this phase of the data analytics project. It sometimes requires more time to understand, locate, acquire, and clean data than to build the analytical model.

Below are some common causes of "dirty" data:

- **Data could be missing.** Most models and analytical methods don't have any way of dealing with missing data, so it's important to fill it in or remove it.
- **Some of the data could be outliers.** An outlier is a number that is considerably and suspiciously larger or smaller than the rest of the numbers within the same KPI. For example, if most reps have a tenure of 0 to 20 years, then a tenure of 100 years is definitely an outlier.
- **The data may have to be scaled.** If one of the variables ranges from 0 to 100, while another variable ranges from –1 to 1, many models will misinterpret the first variable as being about 100 times more important than the second, even though that is not necessarily true. One way to normalize is to divide every entry in the first KPI by

100, scaling it down to a level comparable to the second variable.

There are other types of data cleaning and standardizations that need to be done, but they are certainly too numerous to list here.

AN ITERATIVE PROCESS

Data analytics is an iterative process. Improvements are always possible. For example, given enough time, the team might be able to identify KPIs that are better than the ones they have chosen, or they might be able to agree on better types of data to collect. But they're not trying to achieve the optimum *possible* solutions. Their goal is to achieve the optimum *practical* solutions within given time and resource constraints. As you proceed in a methodical way, often by trial and error, you will get closer and closer to this goal.

Data analytics takes much of the guesswork out of decision making. It helps you to intelligently determine the best course of action and to measure the effectiveness of your actions once taken. The data itself isn't the answer. The data is only valuable when it provides insights. If the data you have gathered doesn't provide the insights you need to make your decisions, gather and analyze more data.

FAMILIARITY VS. TECHNICALITIES

Now that you have all this technical detail to chew on, I want to make one final, important point. Our team of soon-to-be heroes is learning that analytics is only as valuable as the business knowledge it is based on. "The predictive power of big data, when applied to human behavior, is set to revolutionize how business operates," says researcher and journalist Vikram Choudhury.[2] "[But] vast resources of information are meaningless without intelligent interpretation. ... "

Analytics itself is a commodity. You can "buy" the services of a data statistician anywhere these days. What you can't buy is someone who knows your business and can ask the right questions. You need one or more people on your team who understand the business and can interpret the data and results of the analysis as they apply to your business.

The best partner for a data scientist is someone who is both knowledgeable about the business and relentlessly curious about what makes it tick. This type of person knows how to ask the right questions and judge whether data (input or output) "feels right." That's another good reason for building an internal analytics capability. Deep knowledge of your company, combined with data analytics prowess, is a winning combination.

NOTES

1. www.balancedscorecard.org
2. *People Matters* magazine, September 2013

Chapter 5

DESCRIBING WHAT HAPPENED

When she arrived at work early the next morning, Stacy was surprised to see Henry seated at the conference table where their taskforce had met the previous afternoon. He was even wearing the same clothes from the day before, and he seemed so much at home in the space that she felt a bit like she was intruding. "Good morning, Henry."

"Morning?" a startled Henry said, as he looked out the window. "Oh, right, so it is. Here, look at these." He pushed a stack of reports across the table. "I made about fifty charts of different slices of the data you gave me, and even though we need a lot more, I was able to dig up some good stuff." He pointed to a chart on the top of the stack that showed an inverted pyramid (see Figure 5.1).

"This chart is our pipeline," continued Henry. "It shows what typically happens to the leads generated by marketing. On average, only 80 percent make it through the qualification stage. That's a 20 percent loss. We lose 5 percent more during the prospecting stage of the sales process, another 10 percent lost during the discovery and demo stage. We lose another 20 percent between stages 2 and 3, so only 45 percent of the total leads we began with make it to the proposal stage. That's a huge loss! And by the time we get through the negotiation and contract stages, only 20 percent of our original leads are won."

"This confirms what I've suspected," said Stacy. "We knew our win rate was only 20 percent, but now we know we should look into why so many of our leads are lost between stages 2 and 3, and between 3 and 4. Besides, I know our

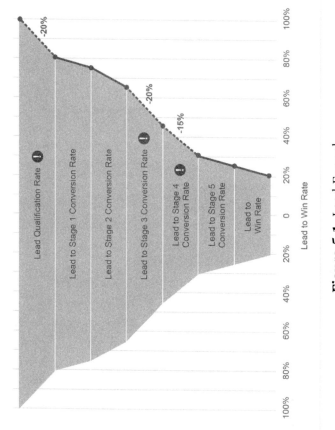

Figure 5.1 Lead Funnel

average pipeline is only three times larger than our quota, which is pretty bad. No wonder we're not making quota. With a 20 percent win rate, our pipeline needs to be five times larger than our quota. If we want to actually *increase* our revenues by 30 percent, we need to increase our pipeline to quota ratio to at least 6.5x. Considering where we are, that'll be a huge challenge!"

Henry agreed, "Also look at our average deal size." He placed a chart with the heading. "Average Deal Size, Win Rate" in front of Stacy (see Figure 5.2).

"The numbers on the left vertical axis are average deal size," Henry explained, "and the bars show the revenue for the two different types of accounts: revenue to new customer accounts, or new business, and revenue to existing customer accounts, or upsell. The bar on the left shows that the average deal size for new accounts is $200,000, and the bar on the right shows that the average deal size for existing accounts is only $50,000. That's a huge difference!"

"Sounds like we should be focusing more on new accounts?" pondered Stacy.

"Maybe, but let's dig in a bit more so we know we have the right answer for the right reason," said Henry. "Remember, we're just at the descriptive analytics stage, and these charts only tell us *what* has happened, not *why*. We'll know more about 'why' when we get to the diagnostic analytics stage. But for now, we don't want to let these initial results give us a false sense of confidence about our ability to plan strategy. It's a rookie mistake." Henry said with a confident wink.

"Is there any deeper meaning behind the Win Rate line?" asked Stacy, pointing to the overlaid line that trended up from

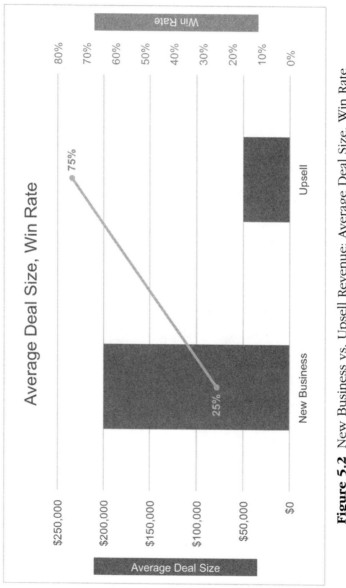

Figure 5.2 New Business vs. Upsell Revenue: Average Deal Size, Win Rate

left to right. "Notice that the win rate is only 25 percent for new accounts," said Henry, "but it's 75 percent for existing accounts. Given that the probability of winning upsell deals is so much higher, it seems we shouldn't neglect our existing customer accounts. There's opportunity there to harness our current relationships to add more value to existing customers. Good for them and good for us." Next, Henry referred to a chart labeled "% Revenue Contribution" (see Figure 5.3).

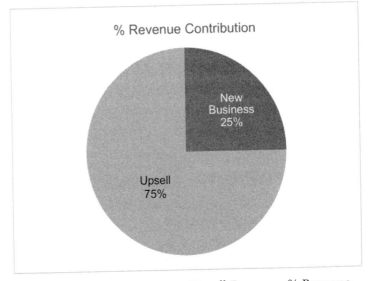

Figure 5.3 New Business vs. Upsell Revenue: % Revenue Contribution

"Upsell deals contribute 75 percent of our overall revenues," Henry went on, "so they're clearly very important. But you're right when you say that we should put more emphasis on new business, because the average size of new deals is so much higher. Let's take a closer look at deal size."

He slid a document labeled "Deal Distribution and Win Rate" across the table to Stacy (see Figure 5.4). "The bars represent the number of deals in each deal size category. By referring to the left vertical axis, you can tell that 300 of our deals were in the $10,000 to $20,000 category, and 200 deals were in the $20,000 to $50,000 category."

"That's about half of the 1,000 or so deals represented on this chart," said Stacy.

"Right," said Henry. "I suspected that the figure of $100,000 for an average deal size might be misleading, so I looked at the median. It's only $20,000. In other words, half of our deals are $20,000 or less."

"Then it does look like we do have a deal-size problem," said Stacy. "Only about 100 deals out of 1,000 were valued at $1 million or more. And what does that downward trend line overlaid on the bars represent?"

"That's the win rate," said Henry. "It relates to the percentages on the right vertical axis. We win about 65 percent of the deals valued at $10,000 or less, we win 50 percent of the $10,000 to $20,000 deals, but only about 5 percent of the largest deals. In other words, the reps who work on the largest deals are wasting their time and coming away empty-handed 95 percent of the time."

"Good morning! You two data-birds seem to be hard at work."

Henry and Stacy looked up to see Jim Forrester standing in the doorway.

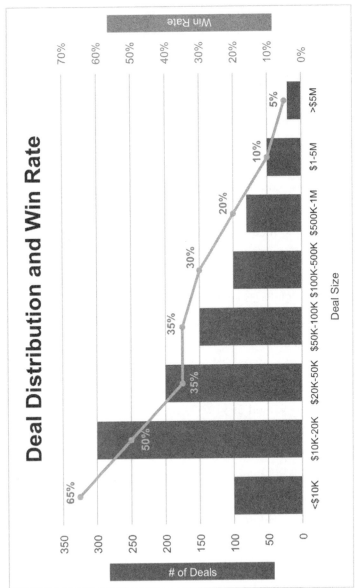

Figure 5.4 Deal Distribution and Win Rate

"What brings you into our plush world headquarters?" said Stacy said to Jim, changing the subject. "You're supposed to be out slaying dragons in the real world."

"I came in to help train some new reps in Sales Boot Camp class, and Cathie came along to make sure I don't tell jokes the whole time," said Jim with a smile. "Thought we'd drop by to say hello."

"I'm glad you did," said Stacy. "Take a look at these reports Henry made."

Jim and Cathie sat down, and Henry gave them a guided tour through a few of the reports. When they were finished, Jim turned to Stacy: "You're a numbers person. What do you think?"

"I'm intrigued," Stacy replied. "But Henry has convinced me that it's too early to make any decisions about what actions to take, so I think we should keep looking at the data."

"And we have plenty more data to look at. These reports are only early indicators. Future reports should become more rich and meaningful. Check this one out," Henry said as he laid a chart titled "Revenue Contribution and Win Rate by Product" in front of the group (see Figure 5.5). "The bar graph shows the relative revenue contributions of our various products. The line overlay shows the win rate percentage for each product."

"Wow!" said Stacy. "We've always focused on the revenue contributions of our top-selling products on our sales ops reports, but we've paid very little attention to our low-sellers. Look at these high win rates for products G and H. Putting these two data sets on the same report paints a whole different picture."

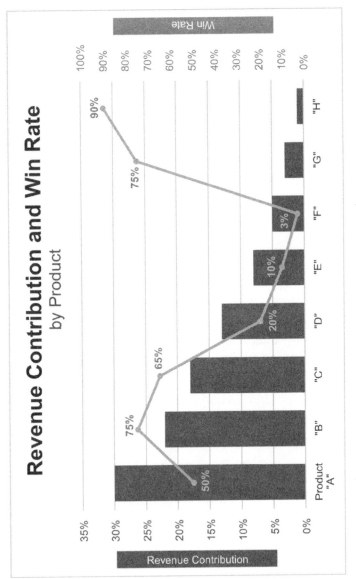

Figure 5.5 Revenue Contribution and Win Rate

"My enablement team has done very little training on products G and H because their sales have been so low," added Cathie. "But considering their high win rates, perhaps we should reevaluate that."

"Our competitors are doing very well with their products in those categories," added Jim. "Maybe we put more emphasis on selling products G and H with spiffs, incentives, and awareness campaigns, and if enablement did some more training on them, we could bring their revenue numbers up fast."

"I knew that product A accounted for about 30 percent of our total revenue, and that products A, B, and C together accounted for about 70 percent," said Stacy, "but I never thought to bring that up for discussion. This seems to indicate that we should focus more effort on those three products."

"I like your thinking," said Cathie. "Along those same lines, perhaps we should deemphasize products E and F. We sell those products to more mature markets, so there are fewer growth opportunities. Maybe we should even consider phasing them out or selling them off to some other company."

"Let's not write them off too quickly," said Stacy. "We spent quite a bit of money developing them. Let's dig deeper to see what's driving these win rates."

"Stacy's right," said Henry. "It's too early to make decisions; let's keep uncovering insights. Here's another." He laid a report titled "Rep Attainment Distribution" on the table (see Figure 5.6).

"This is depressing!" said Jim. "It's bad enough that only 20 percent of our reps are making quota, but this really paints a dismal picture. Seventeen percent of our reps are at 24 percent of quota or less, and 26 percent are between 25 percent and

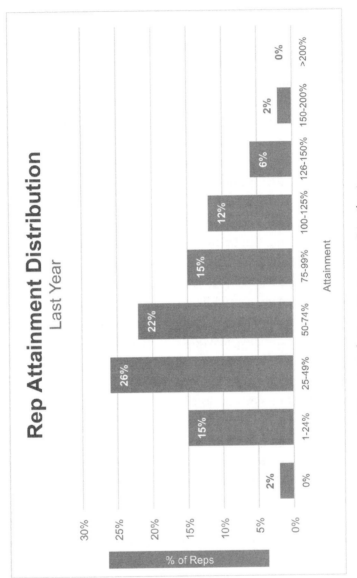

Figure 5.6 Rep Attainment Distribution

49 percent. This is way below the reported benchmarks for our industry."

"I'd like to know how many of the reps who are below quota have taken training," said Cathie. "I'll bet it's a pretty low percentage. Why is it always such a fight to get them to take the training they need?"

"Henry, could we see the same report by geographic region?" asked Stacy. "I know from experience that enablement can vary by location. And how about by tenure? My hunch is that reps who've been here longer are selling more, but it would be interesting to know for sure."

"I'm quite sure our numbers weren't this bad in the past," said Jim. "Maybe all those new hires are pulling down our averages."

"I've been fighting to get more budget to revamp new hire boot camp," said Cathie. "Maybe if Pam saw this graph she'd find the funding."

"Wow, I'm sorta getting the sense that you guys are getting excited about data analytics," said Henry, giving Cathie, Stacy, and Jim a smile. "It's always good to have new converts to our benevolent cult."

"Yeah, I'm beginning to feel like Billy Beane!" said Jim. "You know, *Moneyball*, about how Beane transformed the Oakland A's from losers to winners using data analytics? It's a great story, and maybe we can do the same thing here at Trajectory."

"Good work, Hank," Jim said, patting Henry on the back.

"That last chart on attainment makes me even more curious about what factors are impacting our win rate," said Stacy. "Henry, do you have any magical charts for that?"

"Glad you asked," said Henry, handing Stacy a chart titled "Top Reasons for Lost Deals" (see Figure 5.7). "I ran this report to see why we lose deals, and I was pretty surprised to see that 62 percent are due to customer abandonment. That seems high."

"What? Customer abandonment? That can't be right." Cathie looked puzzled. "How could more than half our deals go south on account of the customer just walking away and not buying from anyone? That's almost worse than losing to a competitor. It's really a waste of time."

"Wow! I knew we had deal-qualification issues, but I never realized how serious they were," said Stacy. "Our managers need to be doing a better job of holding our reps accountable for how they use their time and what kind of deals they work on."

"Yes, it seems that our reps are wasting hours and hours of precious time chasing deals that are never going to close, either for us or our competitors," added Jim. "We've always collected data about the deals we lose to our competitors, but we haven't paid as much attention to the deals that customers abandon, so I never realized we had such a big deal-qualification issue. But we shouldn't necessarily blame our sales managers for allowing our reps to pursue bad leads. They need more tools and training about how to coach reps and hold them accountable."

"Henry, can we figure out what kind of deals are usually abandoned?" asked Cathie. "If so, we can use that information to teach our managers how to better coach and support the reps, and we can teach our reps how to do a better job of

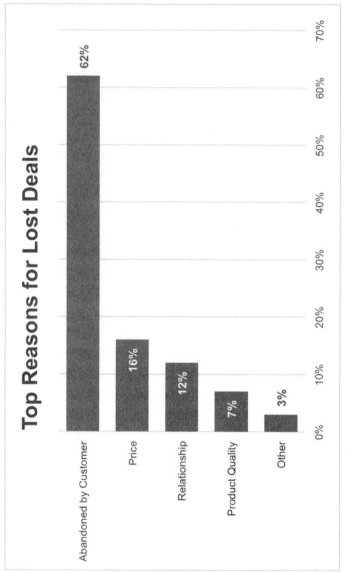

Figure 5.7 Top Reasons for Lost Deals

forecasting. On the most basic level, even a deal-qualification checklist could help the reps and their managers."

"Well, the good news is that we don't lose many deals because of poor product quality," Jim continued. "Product changes are the toughest nut to crack. If it turns out that pricing is a major issue, we can fix that more easily. We don't want to discount ourselves out of healthy margins, but we also don't want to lose high-value accounts on account of price."

"If relationships are a top barrier for our sales reps, that's something we can address with training," added Cathie. "I keep reading about courses that specifically teach reps how to more successfully interact with C-level executives. It may be that our reps could build stronger relationships with partners. This data is giving me a long list of potential fixes to our issues."

Henry nodded with a satisfied look: "You guys are on a roll. I can't wait to show this stuff to Pam."

Forty-five minutes later, Pam was just getting off the phone when Stacy, Cathie, and Henry appeared at her office door. She motioned them in and Henry proceeded to guide her through the charts.

"Well, that gives me a better understanding of some of the problems we face," Pam said, after Henry had finished his presentation. "But I still have questions. How do we know which of these charts to focus on? And what actions will give us the highest return on investment? We need to prioritize our efforts, so we can better understand why so few of our reps are making quota. That seems to me to be the key problem to fix."

"If we can figure out what the successful reps are doing right, maybe we can teach their tricks to the underperformers," suggested Cathie.

"That's a good approach, and I think I can drill down further to identify the most important factors that are preventing reps from making quota," said Henry. "Up to this point, we've just relied on descriptive analytics. It tells us *what* has happened. The next step is diagnostic analytics. That will tell us *why* certain things have happened. If you give me three weeks and access to the right data, I should be able to produce some insightful reports."

"Henry, can I get a breakdown of the top reasons for lost deals at the individual sales rep level?" Cathie asked. "With that information, I should be able to target my training interventions to the reps who most need it."

"I'll do everything I can to help you get the data you need," said Stacy.

"Let me know if you run into any resistance, Henry," said Pam. "I'm here to back you up. Jim and I need to go over this with Joe. Any changes we ultimately make are going to dramatically affect him, and I want him to know we're not trying to cut him out of the decision-making process. Stacy, you and Henry use the same presentation to update the other members of the taskforce. Tell them to keep this information confidential for the time being."

"I wonder what Joe will think of this," said Stacy. That was the elephant in the room, and Pam and Jim traded a look, both thinking the same thing.

SUMMARY

After the taskforce adjourns late in the evening, Henry works all night producing some initial descriptive analytics reports using data supplied by Stacy. When Stacy, Jim, and Cathie come in the next morning, he shows them some eye-opening reports on pipeline, deal size, win rate, and rep performance. They are particularly stunned to see how many deals are being abandoned by customers. Henry cautions them against jumping to conclusions and trying to plan corrective actions before they have analyzed sufficient data. Pam instructs Stacy and Henry to show the other members of the taskforce what they've found, while she and Jim go over the reports with Joe.

COMMENTARY

As our characters start diving into the data in this chapter, they gain a greater understanding of the factors affecting their business and the dynamics behind the numbers. By asking the right questions and "slicing and dicing" the data, they begin to see the power of analytics. The four levels of analysis diagram discussed in Chapter 2 calls this type of reporting *descriptive analytics.*

Descriptive analytics is a process of discovery that basically asks the question: "What happened?" It generally answers that question by means of reports and dashboards. Although this is the first and least technologically sophisticated of the four levels of analytics, it is still very powerful. As we saw in this chapter's story, a single insight can completely change the direction of a business.

I'm an early student and big fan of Edward Rolf Tufte. He is an American statistician and professor emeritus of political science, statistics, and computer science at Yale University and a pioneer in the fields of information design and data visualization. His books, especially *The Visual Display of Quantitative Information,* have greatly inspired me over the years, and I have on many occasions bought copies for my teams and sent my key leaders to his classes.[1]

One of the key principles that I have learned from Tufte is the power of visual info-graphics to persuade. Even fantastic business insights can fail to impress listeners if only spoken, but an elegant, well-crafted chart will never fail to impact an executive audience.

ABOUT DESCRIPTIVE ANALYTICS

Explanation: The results of descriptive analytics are usually presented as graphical charts or summary statistics (e.g., as averages, means, minimums, and maximums of measured variables) within reports or dashboards. The greatest portion of analytics used in day-to-day business operations is descriptive in nature.

Example: In this chapter, Henry's chart titled "Revenue Contribution and Win Rate" is a great example of the compelling insights descriptive analytics can surface. Henry developed this report by persistent, intelligent exploration.

He began by looking at each variable separately. After seeing that Products A through H had different revenue contributions to the total, he used his understanding of the sales process to ask a logical next question: Do these different products also have different win rates? It turned out that the win rates and revenue contributions did, in fact, have an interesting interrelationship on a product-by-product basis. Once this became clear to Henry, he decided to show the chart to the team.

But not every question yields an interesting answer. If Henry had found that all products convert at approximately the same rates, there would be no reason to show such a mundane result to the team. This is why descriptive analytics can be an unpredictable process. It is possible to construct millions of charts from all the data available, but only a small fraction of them will be interesting or informative, and an even smaller fraction will be meaningful in a business sense.

Insight: A common pitfall of the descriptive analytics process is selection bias. If you have some hypothesis about what's going on in your business, you could almost certainly come up with five charts that support your hypothesis. Many times, however, it would also be possible to come up with other charts that show just the opposite. The danger is that, even without realization or intent, you may find yourself presenting only the charts that support your view. Data packs the power to convince an audience of something that isn't entirely true. Statisticians and others who present data have an ethical responsibility to use this power accurately and fairly.

By the way, descriptive analytics is a broad term, and the reports in Chapter 1 would also fall into this category. However, those reports revealed so little information that some people would prefer to label them descriptive *reporting*.

DATA ANALYTICS: THE REAL GAME-CHANGER

In a blog I wrote for *Forbes*, I talked about how today's tight budgets have subjected the corporate learning and enablement functions to tremendous scrutiny. In the article I mentioned virtual learning (delivering training remotely, usually online), but my key point was about how data analytics can improve the effectiveness of training by helping businesses identify problems, design training programs to address them, and measure the results of their interventions.

After the article was published, I received an email from one of my contacts in another company saying, "Great article! You're right. Virtual learning is the game changer."

It was nice of this guy to write, but I think he missed the point. To me his email indicated just how far there is to go before data analytics is broadly accepted as a game changer. My great hope is that very soon directors of sales enablement everywhere will recognize the game-changing potential of data analytics and take action to be able to quantitatively demonstrate how training programs are increasing sales effectiveness. Once they have done this, they will no longer have to worry about whether they will survive the budget wars. Instead of looking for ways to cut back, they'll be able to focus on doing more.

PRACTICAL CHANGE MANAGEMENT

Change is a prerequisite for progress. Data analytics projects almost invariably require significant organizational change, and resistance to change is the major cause of data analytics failures. Some companies—far too many, actually—devote a great deal of attention to the technical aspects of data analytics, but they overlook the human aspects. As a result, they never implement the recommendations produced by their data analytics team or, if they do, the implementation is unsuccessful. The money and time spent on the initiative are essentially wasted.

Pam instructed Stacy and Henry to socialize their recommendations to the other members of the taskforce before she called everyone together for a meeting. This was wise. No one likes to be caught off-guard by surprises. People are more likely to agree with a proposal if they are afforded the courtesy of an advance personal explanation. This is especially true with analytics, because it often impacts people in a personal way. They need time to study the details and nuances of the proposal before it is implemented.

Until someone has actually experienced its power and benefits, data analytics can seem strange, impersonal, and intimidating. Because it challenges the old ways of doing things, it tends to attract more than its share of skeptics. Some of these skeptics become so threatened that they turn into "internal terrorists" and actually work against the success of an analytics initiative. In our story, Joe Kirsch comes close to being this sort of person.

As an analytics project progresses and the successes accumulate, many people who were previously skeptics become believers. Some will even become ambassadors and champions. When an initiative goes well, the culture eventually becomes so aligned with the project's goals that terrorists can't survive.

Problems arise when the leaders of a data analytics initiative do not practice effective change management principles. The recommendations that a data analytics initiative produces may require changes to longstanding processes and procedures, which can then affect the whole culture of an organization. Almost always a few people are adversely affected, at least in their own judgment. Implementing these types of transformational changes requires strong, thoughtful leadership.

If you are planning to play a leadership role in implementing a data analytics initiative, here are some principles you may want to keep in mind:

- Gain buy-in from the beginning by talking to everyone involved and inviting their participation. People need to hear something several times to become comfortable with new ideas, and they need private space to process the change.

- Understand the Kubler-Ross Change Curve (sometimes called the change acceptance curve)—where you came from, where you are, and what's coming up next in your change journey.[2]
- Include detractors in the inner circle of your team. Consider making your biggest detractor your chief lieutenant. If warranted, hold him or her accountable for successfully carrying out assigned change-related responsibilities.
- Search for people who can be helpful. Be a connector. Conduct skip-level meetings all over the organization. Don't simply recruit people according to title or position. Look for the influencers and people who are doing amazing, cool, impactful work. Pam finds Henry rather accidently because she admired his car, but typically you will find the people you need by asking around.

WHY DESCRIPTIVE IS NOT ENOUGH

Descriptive analytics can produce charts with compelling insights, but don't stop there. Push forward with the processes of discovery, forecasting, and planning by using the power of diagnostic, predictive, and prescriptive analytics.

Descriptive analytics often will surface some very helpful insights, but it can also tempt managers to draw erroneous conclusions that could lead to unproductive actions. Why? Because descriptive analytics does not employ statistical algorithms designed to answer the questions of *why* the data says what it does and *which* variables are most influential. We'll talk about techniques that provide answers to these questions in subsequent chapters.

NOTES

1. www.edwardtufte.com/tufte/books_vdqi.
2. www.exeter.ac.uk/media/universityofexeter/humanresources /documents/learningdevelopment/the_change_curve.pdf

Chapter 6

DIAGNOSING WHAT'S WRONG

Joe Kirsch spent about twelve seconds looking over the spreadsheet in front of him before the veins startled pulsing in his head. Finally, in measured tones, he bristled: "I don't need some kid coming in here fresh out of college telling me how to run my sales force. My gut instincts work better than any spreadsheet."

Pam had expected an adverse reaction, but now she understood just why Jim had suggested they meet Joe, the VP of North America sales, in Trajectory's crowded company cafeteria.

"Joe, these are just preliminary ideas," Pam explained. "There will be more discussion before we implement anything new. Jim and I just wanted to bring you in the loop, so we can incorporate your feedback."

"I don't want to know any more about the latest fad," said Joe. "The whole process is a waste of time."

"I get it," interjected Jim. "I had doubts myself. But I think data analytics is right. The way we're talking about things make a lot of sense."

"Jimbo, you've only been with Trajectory for two years, I've been here for twelve," countered Joe, pulling a power move. Of course, Pam realized this was a not so subtle jab at her own short tenure. "I've seen new leaders come in and try to implement ideas that worked for them at their previous companies," continued Joe, "and they failed, because these new people didn't understand our culture. I understand this company, and I know how to solve our sales problem. If we're going to make our revenue goals, we need more reps, more competitive products, and better support from marketing. You should see the leads we get! Our lead-gen team gives us lousy deals to pursue. But nobody listens to me."

"Joe, clearly you know a lot about this company," Pam said calmly. "You have great relationships with customers, and your approach was spot-on to get Trajectory from where it started to where it is now." Joe's eyes shifted to Pam, curious where she was going with this. "But only operating from your gut without 'data' is dangerous, and this approach won't take Trajectory to where it needs to go." Pam paused to let this sink in. She was genuinely seeking to understand Joe's position and asked: "What is so hard about giving the data a chance?"

"It sends us down the wrong path and if nothing improves, I'm the one who will be called out for non-performance," Joe responded. "For me this is a lose-lose proposition. I think the company really made a mistake by choosing you over me for the CSO role. I earned this position with my dedication and hard-won experience. You're more interested in the newest trend."

In this awkward moment, Jim dropped his head to study the ceramic coffee cup in front of him. Pam remained silent; it was important to let Joe be heard. Joe's affront dramatically upped the stakes, but she preferred this overt approach to his previous passive-aggressiveness. Finally, she spoke: "Joe, if you can get on board with this new mindset, you can really play an important role in what I'm confident will be a big success. You've been a great asset. But if you can't get on board, maybe your run here has come to an end."

Pam remained calm and held Joe's gaze, Jim didn't take his eyes off his mug. Joe stood up and tossed his napkin aside. "I can see my approach is not what you want. I don't want to stay where I'm not appreciated." He took off his badge, tossed it on the table, and walked out of the cafeteria, leaving his lunch tray behind.

Pam sat there in silence for a few moments, reviewing what had just taken place. Then she turned to Jim: "Would you like a promotion?" Jim didn't answer, still a little blown away by the most recent events. Pam continued, "You and I see eye to eye, and I think you can really make things happen. If you're interested, I'd like you to be our new VP of North America sales."

"I'd be honored," Jim replied.

As soon as she returned to her office, Pam called David Craig, Trajectory's CEO, to tell him that Joe had resigned and that she planned to name Jim Forrester as his successor. She spent the rest of the afternoon speaking personally with each member of the sales leadership team to make sure there were no additional defections. She then sent out an announcement about the personnel changes.

Over the next three weeks, Pam periodically checked in with Henry about the status of the data-crunching. To help him deal with the huge data-quality issues he was encountering, she arranged for blanket approval for all of the support and resources he needed, including approval to purchase some external customer-related data. Finally, the day came for Henry to present his findings to the taskforce. This was a crucial point in the life of the project, and Pam had been eagerly anticipating his presentation.

"Pam asked me to identify the most important KPIs impacting sales, and to figure out why only 20 percent of our reps are making or exceeding quota," Henry began. "As this first slide shows, for each rep I was able to identify more than

137 variables, or KPIs, from seven different data sources" (see Figure 6.1).

Figure 6.1 Sales Rep/KPI Performance Analysis

"For this analysis I had to switch my focus slightly. When we constructed the original KPI map, we looked at all of the variables that impact total rep bookings. But because every rep has a different quota, for this analysis I had to measure impact by percentage of attainment achieved, rather than by actual dollars. That allows us to compare all of the reps 'apples to apples.' Here's the chart I showed to you a few weeks ago" (see Figure 6.2).

"Based on this performance data, I divided the reps into three groups: bottom, middle, and top performers. Bottom corresponds to 0 percent to 49 percent attainment; middle

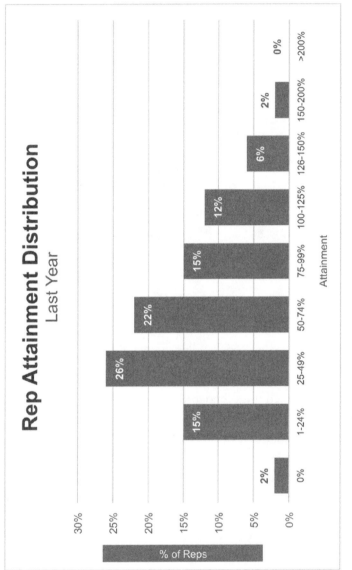

Figure 6.2 Rep Attainment Distribution

corresponds to 50 to 99 percent; and top corresponds to 100 percent attainment or more. Then I determined which KPIs most impact rep attainment. That allowed me to see what the top performers do differently from the bottom performers. The process I used to arrive at this information is too involved to go into now, but I'll be glad to explain it to you later if you like. This chart shows the ten key variables ranked from top to bottom according to their influence" (see Figure 6.3).

"Of the 137 variables impacting rep attainment, it turns out that the most important is the number of unique products a rep sells. Above-average reps sold the complete range of products, while below-average reps restricted themselves to selling a few products they had mastered. The next most important variable is engagement with partners. Above-average reps typically engaged heavily with partners, and even worked with them on new business deals, whereas below-average performers relied only on leads generated by our internal marketing department."

Raj jumped in: "If any of you are concerned about how I might take this remark, relax. What Henry says is true. I can see that our more junior reps don't hustle to prospect and get leads on their own; all they do is take the leads we give them. Our best reps work with partners and hardly use marketing-generated leads at all."

"The third most important variable is average deal size," Henry went on. "The deals closed by above-average performers were almost eight times the size of those closed by below-average performers. Larger deal size is usually a result of selling more products per deal and closing deals with larger new accounts."

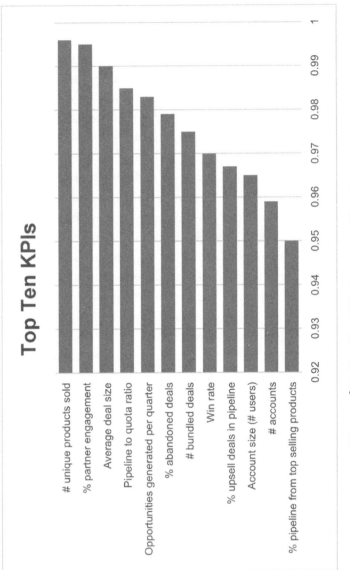

Figure 6.3 Top Ten KPIs Impacting Rep Attainment

Jim leaned over to Pam: "Thanks for the new job, by the way. I won't let you down." Pam smiled, it was a no-brainer for her. She knew she needed to get the entire team moving in the same direction, and Jim was just the guy to do it.

"Pipeline to quota ratio is the fourth most important variable," continued Henry. "Above-average reps tend to maintain a steady rate of opportunity creation throughout the year, except possibly in quarter four. Their pipeline creation per month is almost four times the team average, and their average pipeline was worth seven times their quota. As we move down the chart, you can see that the fifth most important KPI tells us that above-average sales reps have fewer abandoned deals."

Pam looked around at her leadership team. Everyone was taking notes. She could feel the excitement in the air.

Henry continued: "Allow me to show you the full comparison. I call this "Sales Rep DNA." This chart compares the profile of the top sales performers to the profile of the lower performers (see Figure 6.4)."

"Then I went ahead and charted out how each individual rep did last year on each of the top KPIs. This gave me a detailed view of the key strengths and weaknesses of each sales person. Here's a chart that shows data on the ten KPIs for seven randomly chosen reps, numbers 81 through 87 (see Figure 6.5)."

"Interestingly, not all of the below-average reps have the same weaknesses. Let's take rep number 85 as an example. At first glance, it looks like this rep is struggling and needs some help. But there's a silver lining: even though number 85 has only one above-average KPI, out of all the reps shown, he or she is the only one who has an above-average score for the KPI labeled 'Opportunities generated per quarter.' Looks like

Sales Rep DNA
Top vs. Bottom Performers on Top 10 KPIs

	Top Performers	Bottom Performers
# unique products sold	12	4
% partner engagement	65%	32%
Average deal size	$250,000	$120,000
Pipeline to quota ratio	2	0.7
Opportunities generated per quarter	3	1
% abandoned deals	22%	43%
# bundled deals	47	12
Win rate	55%	16%
% upsell deals in pipeline	20%	55%
Account size (# users)	10,000	1500
# accounts	7	3
% pipeline from top selling products	29%	4%

Figure 6.4 Sales Rep DNA

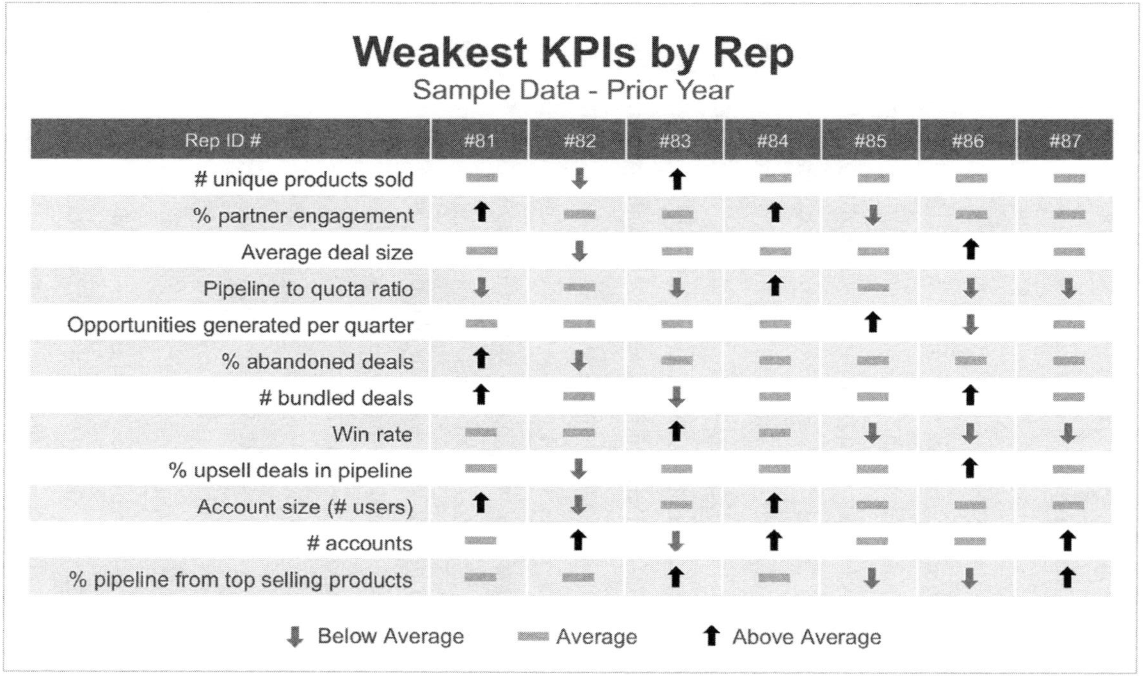

Weakest KPIs by Rep
Sample Data - Prior Year

Rep ID #	#81	#82	#83	#84	#85	#86	#87
# unique products sold		→	↑				
% partner engagement	↑			↑	→	↑	
Average deal size		→				→	→
Pipeline to quota ratio	→		→			→	↑
Opportunities generated per quarter		→			↑		
% abandoned deals	↑		→			↑	↑
# bundled deals	↑		↑			↑	
Win rate		→	↑		→	↑	↑
% upsell deals in pipeline						↑	
Account size (# users)	↑	→	→	↑			↑
# accounts		↑	↑	↑			↑
% pipeline from top selling products					→	→	↑

↑ Below Average   ― Average   ↑ Above Average

Figure 6.5 Weakest KPIs by Rep

everyone else could learn something about generating opportunities from 85." With that, Henry wrapped up his presentation. Everyone was dumbstruck.

Pam broke the ice. "Team, what do you think of Hank's proposal??"

Suddenly the room was abuzz with chit-chat. "I'm going to immediately get enablement focused on helping the average and below-average performers sell high-potential product sets," said Cathie. "We can produce materials on how to better engage with partners, and we'll make the courses on prospecting mandatory. Oh, and a number of reps have said that they didn't get much out of our training. They said they already knew the material. So I'm thinking a one-size-fits-all approach doesn't work. This data will allow us to customize our training to each rep's exact needs. It'll also make it easier to measure the results, because we'll be working on strengthening specific KPIs."

"And I'll direct our reps to immediately start working with partners on joint account planning," said Jim. "I wonder whether we could do the same analysis on our partners. That could be pretty insightful."

"If we have that data, we can customize partner enablement as well," added Cathie. "We could even develop a training program around how to sell effectively through partner relationships."

"Our sales partners use the same CRM, so I don't see any reason why we couldn't do this analysis for them," said Stacy. "For sure, there's an opportunity to improve how we're training them."

"We can spend more of our marketing budget on messages specifically targeted to C-level executives of larger companies," suggested Raj. "That should help increase deal size. We can also focus more marketing dollars on existing accounts to increase upsell. And because the abandonment rate is so high, we need to reevaluate our lead qualification criteria. I've been meaning to address the abandonment issue, but there have been competing priorities. The data says I need to make this a high priority. So I will."

Then Stacy shared some thoughts. "In sales ops we should maintain a leader board that shows the value pipeline each rep creates per month. Then we can collaborate with sales managers to follow up on pipeline creation." She turned to Cathie, "You mentioned when we first looked at the abandoned deal data a few weeks ago that we could create a deal-qualification checklist. How quickly can we get that going?"

"Actually, I've already started working on an analysis that will tell us the key variables behind abandoned deals," Henry interjected. "We'll have essentially the same data for abandoned deals as we have for overall sales."

"This is very exciting," declared Pam. She was delighted to see how the ideas were bubbling up. These people were working as a team.

"It gets even better," said Henry. "We started off by doing descriptive analytics, which gave us a basic assessment of *what* happened. We've just been doing diagnostic analytics, which tells us *why* certain things have happened. The next step is predictive analytics, which will help us predict what *will* happen given certain conditions. For example, if we keep tracking performance, we can forecast who's going to meet quota."

"Are you sure about that?" said Pam. "I don't want to start chasing rabbits."

"Based on what I've seen so far," said Henry. "I can't tell you yet how accurate the predictions will be, but I'm sure we can get valuable results with a reasonable amount of effort. However, we need time to collect the data. The charts I have shown you are based on last year's sales performance. To predict how our reps are going to do for this entire year, we'll need current-year data through quarter two."

"How will that help us?" asked Raj.

"After we're grounded in predictive analytics and have built a model that predicts who will make quota and who won't, we can progress up to prescriptive analytics, which will help us plan strategies," said Henry. "But it's too early to think about that. You guys have plenty to work with for now."

"Okay, Henry," said Pam, "go ahead and set up the predictive analytics model. Everyone else, I want you to start working on your big 'aha' discoveries. Do your best to calculate the anticipated revenue gain from these initiatives, and estimate the additional cost you'll need to execute your proposed ideas. If you can demonstrate a worthwhile ROI, I'll find the funding. What do you say? Are we all in?"

"It makes me nervous, but mostly in a good way," answered Stacy. The others nodded in agreement.

"Then here's what we're going to do," said Pam. "Stacy, I want you to reserve a conference room on this floor for six months. That will be our war room. You and Henry will practically live in there. Let's also plan to meet here weekly for status updates. And everybody should drop by as often as you can to keep the momentum and teamwork going. Stacy, I want you to keep a running log in a secure site online, where the leadership team can access it. That way we all can keep up-to-date on what's been decided and what we've done. And remember, keep this confidential for now."

As people exited the room, there was a sense of excitement. The direction felt right. It was a relief to finally have solid information explaining what had been going wrong. Pam had a sense that if they could impact the right KPIs, success would soon follow. The sales department was on the move, and that was a welcome change.

SUMMARY

Over lunch in the company cafeteria, Pam and Jim try to get Joe to open his mind to the data analytics initiative, but Joe becomes contentious and resigns from the company. Pam promotes Jim to be the new VP of North America Sales. Three weeks later, at the next sales leadership meeting, Henry presents an analysis that identifies the top ten variables (KPIs) that affect sales performance. The top three are (1) number of unique products sold, (2) percentage of partner involvement, and (3) average deal size.

Based on this information, Cathie (enablement), Jim (sales), Stacy (sales ops), and Raj (marketing) come up with ideas about what they plan to do to improve rep performance. Henry says he will develop a predictive analytics model that will predict which reps will make quota for the current year. Pam enthusiastically gives everyone permission to proceed and promises to find budgets for any initiatives that will yield an acceptable ROI that is verifiable by data. She tells Stacy to set up a "war room" to serve as the hub for their activities in the coming months.

COMMENTARY

Diagnostic analytics has helped Pam's team identify the major sales problem areas and which KPIs they should focus on to achieve the greatest impact on the top line. Because everyone is making decisions based on common data rather than on individual intuition, the culture is more aligned, transparent, and cooperative. Strategic actions and multi-functional teamwork have superseded the territorial, blame-shifting, and excuse-making attitudes that characterized previous sessions.

Meanwhile, Pam is fully supporting the new initiatives. When possible, she maintains existing procedures while installing new systems, so as to avoid alienating stakeholders. For example, she tells Raj to continue to operate his lead-generation system in parallel with the new system Henry is developing, even though there have been many complaints about it. Especially with something as complex as data analytics, it's important to introduce and test alternatives gradually before abandoning current systems.

In this chapter, we introduced another critical piece of the data analytics puzzle: Rep DNA. This is a term Henry and the others use to describe the variables, or KPIs, that most strongly influence a particular rep's skills and behaviors. When the rep and the rep's managers know what these strengths and weaknesses are, they can introduce corrective and supportive actions to improve performance, for the benefit of the individual and the organization. This is similar to the doctor analogy mentioned in the Chapter 1 commentary, except that this time the rep, rather than the entire organization, is the patient.

Of course, another dramatic development in this chapter is the resignation of Joe Kirsch. His reaction was extreme, but I crafted it this way for dramatic effect. Typically, this conversation is better had in private, not a crowded company cafeteria, especially if a tantrum is a potential outcome. But Pam did the right thing. She kept her cool, was level-headed and respectful, and showed strength when challenged. In the end a critical barrier to advancing the team and the company was removed, which was probably long overdue.

Some years ago, I was in an executive forum with the top 100 or so leaders at Sun Microsystems. In the Q&A session, CEO Jonathan Schwartz was asked what advice he had for us that he had learned from his own career. He said to make leadership changes as soon as you know they need to be made. You will almost never change your mind from your original impression, so don't drag it out. Sometimes change management means changing the guard. "If you can't get people to change, change the people." Make the call, move on.

ABOUT DIAGNOSTIC ANALYTICS

Explanation: As we pointed out in Chapter 5, descriptive analytics can surface interesting or unexpected results that raise important questions, such as "Which team is the most effective and why?" or "Which variables are the most important to focus on?" These questions can often be answered very effectively by diagnostic analytics, a powerful methodology discussed in this chapter.

The choice of analytical tools will largely depend on the nature of the problem to be diagnosed. Just as Henry used a variety of tools to come up with Trajectory's list of top variables, you will need to choose one or more tools for your specific problem.

Example: Diagnostic analytics can take many forms. In this chapter, Henry defined an output variable (bottom, top, or middle attainment group) and assembled a dataset of input variables (KPIs and other variables that affect KPIs) to determine which ones impacted the output variable and to what degree. To find out which input variables were most influential, he first used some statistical tests to quantify the impact each input variable individually had on the output variable. But these tests were not powerful enough to measure the impact that pairs and larger sets of input variables had on the output variable, so Henry broke out the big guns: his knowledge of machine learning.

If your eyes glaze over when you read "machine learning," fear not. In a nutshell, machine learning is the study of models that learn from data. Once a machine learning model has been "trained" with data, it can be thought of as a fancy black box with input and output terminals. Give the machine learning black box some input variables (also called features), and it figures out what the output should be.

Henry trained a black box that had 137 variables as input and attainment group (bottom, middle, top) as output. Then, in a manner of speaking, he unscrewed the instrumentation panel and peeked inside. This enabled him to see how the black box made use of each of the variables.

Henry found that the black box repeatedly used certain variables when determining output, while other variables had little effect. He concluded that the most frequently used variables were also the most important, and he used this information to rank the KPIs according to their significance.

Insight: A common analytics mistake during the diagnostic process is to confuse correlation with causation. Sometimes we can decisively conclude that a causal relationship exists, but often we simply don't know. In our story, for example, do small deal sizes cause reps to miss their quotas, or are small deal sizes simply correlated with missed quotas? There is no way to tell without running an experiment (also known as an A/B test).

To illustrate, let's say you have 100 reps, and you send half of them to a rep boot camp, while the other half receive no additional training. You can then measure the causal effect of the boot camp by observing the behavior of the two groups of reps over the following quarter. If the reps who went to boot camp show significantly better overall attainment, and there were no other major changes during this period, you can conclude with a high degree of confidence that the boot camp was responsible.

ANSWERING "WHY" WITH QUALITATIVE VS. QUANTITATIVE

Another way to determine which variables are important in differentiating top reps from the others is to simply ask them. Conducting formal interviews can be a great way to gain general insight into how your sales organization functions, but this approach has some serious shortcomings.

Here's a brief illustration of the types of shortcomings you can encounter. I recall a study that looked at what factors make Olympic athletes medalists. Researchers asked medal winners, "What do you think contributed most to your win, other than the amount of training you did?" Many had one thing in common: before the event they spent hours visualizing themselves winning the event and afterwards standing on the podium proudly wearing their medals. The conclusion was that visualization is a key cause of victory.

But interviews with Olympic athletes who did not win a medal uncovered that they, too, spent time visualizing themselves winning the event and standing on the winner's podium. So, for these less successful athletes, visualization obviously didn't help. The original conclusion, based on insufficient data and inadequate analysis, was flawed.

Getting back to sales, this hypothetical example illustrates that in order to properly use qualitative interviews as a diagnostic tool for evaluating rep performance, you would have to interview every rep and attempt to convert verbal responses into actionable conclusions. This would inherently be a subjective process, since both the interviewer and interviewee have unknown biases.

Data analytics, on the other hand, is as objective as the measurements (data) you are able to collect. Objective measurements make for an objective model, and once you have a model developed and vetted, it will be easy to update it with new measurements every quarter.

If you have the time and money to do so, the ideal is to use both quantitative and qualitative methods to gain a deeper understanding of what makes your sales organization tick. Some factors that have a large impact on performance, such as motivation, energy levels, career ambitions, and trust in the company, are difficult to measure quantitatively.

ANALYTICS AND ENABLEMENT: FINALLY, PRECISE GUIDANCE AND REAL RESULTS

Rep DNA is a powerful tool for enhancing the impact of training. It enables sales leaders to pinpoint individual training needs and opportunities; guide the planning, selection, and design of training programs; and provide real business benchmarks to measure progress over the lifecycle of the project.

I've seen companies reap enormous benefits (better early state pipeline, late state pipeline, conversion rate and win rate, stronger brand as an employer of choice, better ability to recruit and retain, and higher employee engagement, just to name a few) from a holistic approach to analytics and enablement that uses steps such as the following:

1. **Inventory Learning Needs.** Analyze rep performance using CRM and other data to identify skills gaps and success drivers, which enablement can use to design training interventions.

2. **Design Learning Programs.** Define business, process, and learning metrics for each sales stage and translate these into core competencies around which enablement can design formal, informal, and social learning programs.

3. **Schedule Learning Programs.** Regularly track sales performance of individual reps on key metrics to identify strengths and weaknesses, and then determine the selection and timing of learning and coaching interventions.

4. **Evaluate Learning Programs.** Design pre- and post-course surveys based on objective metrics related to areas such as prospecting and closing, and use these metrics to measure self-reported confidence (as

contrasted with knowledge assessment) and actual execution against goals.

5. **Prove Business Impact.** Measure pipeline performance (e.g., opportunities created and won, average deal size, sales cycle, win rate, etc.) before and after learning. This step, the brass ring of corporate training, should include quarterly tracking of overall sales performance compared to the company's goals and to the overall market.

Chapter 7

PREDICTING WHAT'S AHEAD

F ive months had passed since the kickoff of the sales data initiative, and the conference room that had been set up as a war room did indeed look like the scene of a battle. Housekeeping had strict orders not to disturb anything in the room, so empty pizza boxes, coffee cups, and soda cans littered a conference table that was piled high with system reports, graphs, charts, and dashboard mockups. All four walls of the room were filled with Dry Erase scribbling, flip-chart paper, and sticky notes.

No one else was in the room at that moment, so Pam sat down at a laptop and scrolled through the wiki of notes and action items that Stacy had kept up-to-date. She was already familiar with all of the entries, but she found it both helpful and satisfying to reread them from time to time to track their progress. She found herself looking at an entry dated April 14:

Henry has informed us that he will need to phase out of his current role by July 31, so he can start his own business. We need to put a big push on finishing the predictive analytics project.

She randomly flipped to the May 2 entry:

Jennifer Chan, B.S. in applied mathematics from MIT and MBA from Stanford, will start in two weeks, as soon as she completes her graduate program. She will assume the role Henry has been playing when Henry leaves. Jennifer will be responsible for building out our internal analytics capability.

"How do you think we're doing, Pam?"

Pam raised her eyes to see Stacy standing over her. She was wearing a big smile and a button on her shirt that read "I Speak Data."

"You probably know better than I do, Stacy. You're in the middle of the battle every day."

"Well, things seem to be going well," said Stacy, taking a seat beside Pam. "Here, I've got some new reports. Look at how our KPIs have changed in the past year" (see Figure 7.1).

"Improvements in every KPI category except deal abandonment," said Pam, eyeing the reports. "It's encouraging to see these increases in number of unique products sold, percentage of deals with partner engagement, and average deal size."

Stacy sang Cathie's praise: "The team she put together to give the reps one-on-one performance coaching on increasing pipeline and product bundling has made a huge difference."

"Did someone mention my name?" asked Cathie, walking in the door.

"We were just talking about the progress you've been making," said Pam.

"Thanks to the data we now have and our new performance coaching program, we've made most of this progress by redirecting resources, without any need for a bigger budget," said Cathie, taking a seat at the table. "Performance coaching has had a side benefit, too. As our coaches work with our top-performing reps, they learn best practices that they pass on to others. This cross-pollination of ideas has given our results another boost."

"That's terrific!" said Pam. "I was impressed by the campaign you created promoting partner engagement. It was

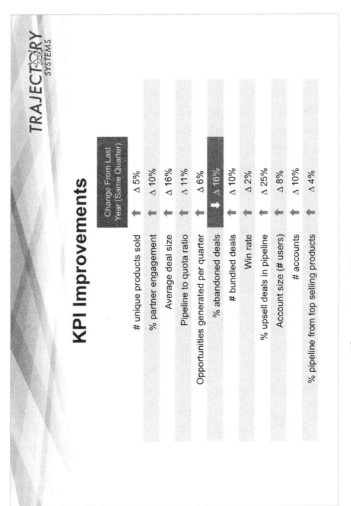

Figure 7.1 KPI Improvements

a nice blend of communication modalities: our online company portal, e-newsletters, and hard-copy marketing collateral."

"We sent out lots of direct pitch emails to the partner community, too," said Cathie. "And we produced videos and launched a social collaboration site dedicated to that group."

"Look at these two reports," said Stacy. "As a result of these marketing campaigns and the additional training, our reps really ramped up their joint deals with partners. The percentage of deals where partners were engaged went up by 10 percent, and the average deal size went up 16 percent" (see Figures 7.2 and 7.3).

"These results prove the importance of working with partners," said Pam. "I can't wait to share these charts with our reps! If you want sales people to pay attention, tell them how they can make more money."

"Enablement isn't done yet," said Cathie. "We're working to customize our partner enablement efforts, so we're developing a formal course on how to sell effectively through partner relationships. We can expect even better results as we move forward."

"Awesome!" said Pam. "Keep up the good work. Any other news?"

"I've got some!" said Jim Forrester, who had just entered the room with Henry and Jennifer Chan. All three took seats at the table, across from Pam and Stacy. "When I first started in this role," Jim continued, "you may remember that I made joint account plans with our ten largest partners. My goal was to get us more aggressively selling to our mutual top accounts. Well, that's starting to pay off. We're beginning to get a significant

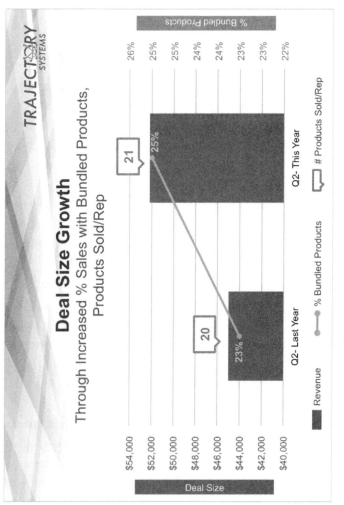

Figure 7.2 Deal Size Growth

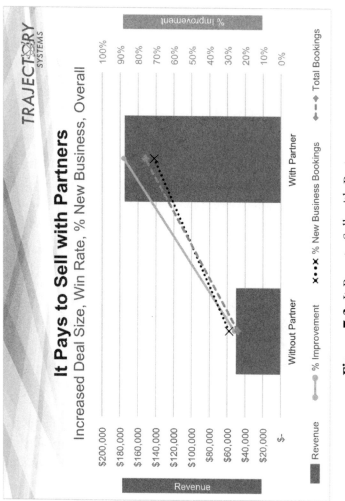

Figure 7.3 It Pays to Sell with Partners

number of high-potential leads with large deal sizes, and it looks pretty good that many of these leads will close by the end of quarter four."

"And the data shows that Raj's campaigns are taking hold," said Stacy. "The major CXO campaign with targeted messages on bundled products is generating leads with large deal sizes. Raj is excited to finally get some solid ROI measurements on the effectiveness of his campaigns. He wants to wait until the end of the quarter to report on that, but I already know the numbers are telling a good story."

"He said he's not certain about his other initiative to improve lead qualification," added Jim. "He configured the lead scoring system in the marketing automation software to help identify high-potential and low-potential leads, but he doesn't have any results yet."

Pam turned to Stacy. "Have you been able to increase the pipeline to quota? I know you've created a leader board that shows how much pipeline each rep creates each month, and the contest you've been running based on it has generated quite a buzz."

"Yes, I borrowed one of Cathie's learning technology wizards and added some gamification elements to the contest," Stacy replied. "And we put the names of the reps' managers on the leader board, too, which really upped the attention reps pay to it. They're scrambling like mad to win the prizes and badges we're awarding each week. CRM entries shot up after we started sharing those results. The best news, of course, is that opportunities increased 6 percent. Here's the latest report" (see Figure 7.4).

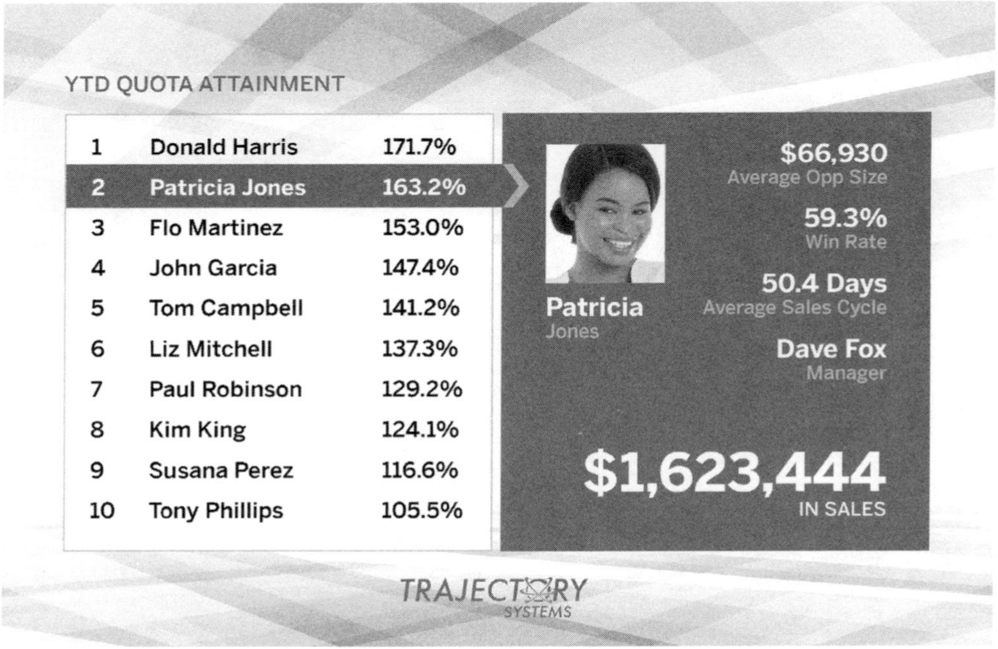

Figure 7.4 Sales Leader Board

"We've also worked with Cathie's team to create and implement a deal-qualification checklist. It will be a few weeks before we see results, but the initial feedback has been very positive."

"It's amazing to see what can happen when we all have good information and pull in the same direction," said Pam, pleased. "Now, what about the brass ring? How are we doing on rep attainment?"

"I think you'll find these next graphs especially interesting," said Stacy. "First, here's last year's data on rep attainment. As the bar on the right shows, only 20 percent of our reps made or exceeded quota" (see Figure 7.5).

"Now look at this. Here's this year's data overlaid on last year's. The bars to the right in each category show the projected rep attainment for this year as a percentage of quota" (see Figure 7.6).

"Your data says we're on track to have 40 percent of our reps meet or exceed quota for the year," exclaimed Pam. "That's a 100 percent increase!"

"I hate to pop balloons at the party," said Jim, "but 40 percent is nothing to write home about."

"I agree," said Stacy, "but look at the shift that's occurring in the entire sales force. The whole curve is shifting to the right, so every category is improving."

"But Stacy, how reliable are these numbers?" Jim sounded concerned.

"We gave them to her," Henry chimed in, smiling broadly at Stacy. "We used previous performance data for reps to train a model that is able to predict with 95 percent accuracy

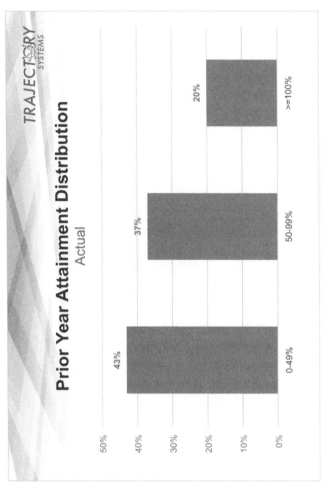

Figure 7.5 Prior Year Attainment Distribution

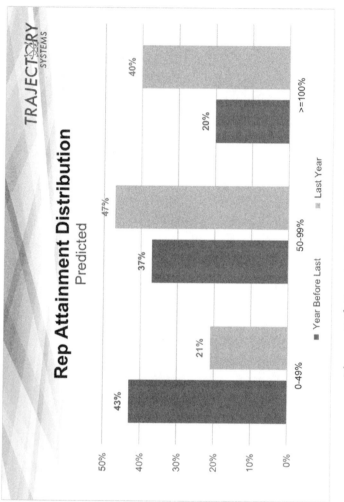

Figure 7.6 Rep Attainment Distribution

whether a rep will be a bottom, middle, or top performer this year. Jennifer can tell you about it."

"We collected data through June of this year on how well each rep actually performed on each of the top ten KPIs," explained Jennifer, "and we ran that data through our trained predictive model, factoring in some seasonal adjustments. The predictive model tells us which attainment group a rep is likely to fall in."

"Keep in mind that this analysis only tells us who is likely to attain quota," added Henry. "It doesn't project how many dollars each rep will book, but we produce that report if anyone wanted it."

"I'd love to see those numbers," said Jim. "By the way, if you can predict bookings by rep, can you also predict total revenue for the year?"

"Yes," said Henry. "We've already started on that. We're using the same approach that we used to determine the DNA of a successful rep to determine the DNA of an ideal deal and the DNA of an ideal account. Using the deal DNA and deal data from previous quarters, we trained predictive models that will tell us which of the deals in the pipe are likely to be won or lost for each rep."

"By extrapolating from this individual information, we can show a realistic valuation of the pipe. Knowing the DNA of a good account will tell us which of the leads and accounts in the territory have a propensity to buy this year, and we can estimate the potential revenue given the opportunity-creation rate of the reps."

"Great!" said Pam. "What about analyzing our partners the way we did our reps? Where does that stand?"

"I've budgeted funds for a project to determine the DNA of our most valuable partners, so we can pursue other partners with those qualities," answered Jim. "Jennifer is going to lead it with guidance from Henry."

"I've developed a set of rules for calculating the purchasing propensity for each prospect," Henry added. "That will allow us to score the incoming leads, so the sales reps can prioritize them and follow up on the ones most likely to close. It will also allow us to calculate the expected value of our pipeline, so we can project what our revenues will be."

"Are you sure we need another lead-scoring system?" asked Jim. "Raj has already set one up. If we get a lead that's signed by a VP or by someone who has been using our free trial version, we give that prospect high priority and pursue him hard."

"The analyses I'm working on will tell us not only which prospects will or won't buy, but also the reasons why," said Henry. "There are many other aspects like firmographics—that's like demographics but for businesses and organizations—news and events, marketing intervention, and prospect actions that can be tracked to understand which factors have the highest correlation to purchase outcome. This will make the predictions more accurate."

"And they'll tell us the reasons why various reps are going to make quota or not," added Pam. "But I don't want to disrupt our current scoring system, so for the foreseeable future we will run it in parallel with the new analytics process."

"This analysis of KPIs will be so helpful to me," said Cathie. "A few months ago I started implementing individualized training plans based on the deficiencies that our analytics revealed, but as usual the reps have been resisting. They keep saying that they don't need more training. But with this data I can point to exactly who needs what, as well as why he needs it. We can individually coach reps in the specific areas where they most need to improve."

"We won't need the compliance stick now that we've got a big carrot," added Jim. "We can simply point out to reps that the best way for them to make quota and get their full commission is to take the training we show them they need."

"I'll go one step further," said Pam. "With this data as convincing evidence, I'll make training mandatory. That will show people that we're serious." She went to the white board and drew three circles. The first she labeled "Right Sales Reps," the second she labeled "Right Deals," and the third "Right Accounts."

"To reach our goals, we need to have the right sales people, which means they have to have the right knowledge, skills, behaviors, and partners," Pam continued. "We also need to have the right deals, which means our products must be competitive and we must do a good job of bundling; and we need to have the right accounts, which means we must do a good job of qualifying leads. This analysis gives us exactly the information we need to have for all three, and when we have all three components, we'll get this." She added an arrow titled "Revenue Success" that pointed to the intersection of all three circles (see Figure 7.7).

"Henry, as soon as you get your new firm set up, send me a proposal. Trajectory just might be your first client; let's see if we can't keep you around here a bit longer," said Pam.

Henry shot Stacy a furtive glance.

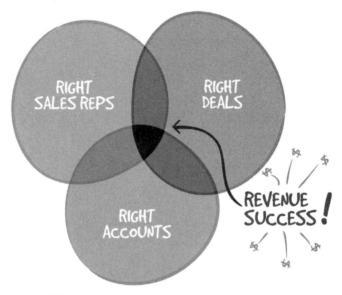

Figure 7.7

SUMMARY

Five months after the kickoff of the data analytics initiative, Pam's team is making good progress by strategically targeting their efforts on the KPIs that promise the greatest return on investment. The data shows improvements across the board, and Stacy, Cathie, and Jim tell Pam that they've been able to increase partnering, pipeline, and deal size, primarily by redirecting already available resources.

Henry has informed Pam that he will need to phase out of his current role by July 31, so he can start his own business. Jennifer Chan, who has a B.S. in applied math from MIT and an MBA from Stanford, has been hired to take over Henry's responsibilities when he leaves. Her overall responsibility will be to build an internal analytics capability.

COMMENTARY

Diagnostic analytics has helped Pam's team identify Trajectory's major sales problems and prioritize corrective interventions. In this chapter the team is using predictive analytics to prioritize specifically which reps need help. For example, once the data pinpointed deal size as a problem, Cathie launched classes and individualized coaching to address it, and Raj supported her efforts with marketing campaigns.

Meaningful data allows Pam and her crew to take strategic actions instead of simply throwing money at the problems. Rather than hire more reps, her people are redirecting available resources, with little or no increases in their overall budgets.

We also see in this chapter that Stacy in sales operations has started to build out the team's internal data analytics capability by hiring Jennifer Chan. She has wisely brought Jennifer on board in time for Henry to mentor her before he leaves to start his own business.

ABOUT PREDICTIVE ANALYTICS

Explanation: Once you have a good sense of what your data is telling you, it may be time to deploy predictive models. Predictive analytics approaches are about using already-collected data to train models that will attempt to generalize to other situations (to new, unseen data).

For example, the program on your computer that handles email probably provides some sort of spam detection. Have you ever wondered how it can detect what is spam and what is not? The people who built that program trained it by feeding it millions of emails, a portion of which were spam and were identified to the model as such. After processing considerable training data, the model's mathematical optimization routines learned to distinguish spam from legitimate email. It was then able to predict which new emails were spam with a rather high degree of accuracy.

Example: In this chapter, Henry used data from the first two quarters of the previous year to train a model that predicts whether a rep will be a bottom, middle, or top performer in terms of attainment percentage in the current year. This predictive model is the same type of machine learning model he used to find the most important variables during the diagnostic analytics stage, but it's used differently. Instead of unscrewing the black box and seeing which variables are crucial, the focus here is on using the outputs of the black box (that is, the predictions) to figure out which reps need the most help.

How did Henry know that this model had acceptable prediction accuracy? He used all of last year's data (not just the first two quarters) to validate! Here's a simplified explanation of his procedure:

First, Henry divided last year's data into four chunks, as follows:

1. KPI data from the first two quarters for half of the reps
2. KPI data from the first two quarters for the other half of the reps
3. Attainment data for the entire year for the same reps as in number 1
4. Attainment data for the entire year for the same reps as in number 2

For the first phase of the training, Henry fed in a half year of KPI data (1) and a full year of attainment data (3) for one set of reps. The model processed this data and "learned" a mathematical relationship between the inputs (KPI data) and the outputs (attainment results).

Understandably, machine learning algorithms are less accurate when analyzing data they have seen before. So, when validating a model in machine learning, the data used to *validate* the model should be different from the data used to *train* the model.

To validate the accuracy of this model, Henry fed six months worth of the prior year's KPI data for the second set of reps (2) into the model and asked the model to predict the attainment data for those reps for the entire year. He then compared the resulting predictions against the true attainment data for this second set of reps for the entire previous year (4). If Henry's black box had operated perfectly, with appropriate adjustments for seasonality, and so forth, the *predicted* attainment for this second set of reps for the entire prior year would have exactly matched their *actual* attainment. Of course, Henry didn't expect such a great outcome, because models are never perfect.

It turned out, nevertheless, that the error rate, which was the difference between the model's predicted attainment for last year and the actual attainment for last year (4), was acceptable. His next step was to *retrain* the model with data from the first half of the prior year for *all* of the reps [(1) and (2)].

After retraining, Henry was eager to use the model for its intended purpose: to predict attainment for all reps for the entire *current* year. He started by feeding actual KPI data for the first two quarters of the current year into the black box. Then he "turned the crank" and the model produced the desired prediction. He had confidence in this prediction, but he wouldn't know for sure how accurate it was until after the end of the year, when he could compare it to the attainment scores reps actually achieved.

Insight 1: Note that, even though we are presenting prescriptive analytics after discussing diagnostic analytics, both use the same fundamental tools. This illustrates a key point: these four stages (descriptive, diagnostic, predictive, and prescriptive) are not necessarily sequential. They're just a helpful way to divide analytics work into manageable chunks.

Insight 2: Predictive analytics isn't guaranteed to "work." When building a predictive system, your data analysts will have to try out different models, measure how well each one performs, and then decide whether to use the model's predictions.

But what should you do if you find during the evaluation period that the model is accurate only 60 percent of the time, and you know that's the best you can realistically expect? Well, the answer depends on the application. If the goal is to decide whether an email is spam, then a 40 percent error rate (identifying 40 percent of good emails as spam) is not nearly good enough for production. But if the goal is predicting whether an important sales deal will fall through, the model may still be useful, even though it may cause some false alarms and fail to call attention to some precarious deals.

For example, imagine that for a particularly important sales deal the model says "there is a 35 percent chance that the deal will fail." Assume that, in response to this insight, you provide extra support for the reps, and the deal goes through. Even if the model was wrong and the deal was as good as signed, the clients will still be impressed by your high level of due diligence, so your extra effort was not wasted.

165

APPLYING PREDICTIVE ANALYTICS TO IMPROVE SALES REP PERFORMANCE

Improving sales reps performance requires more than providing additional training or better leads. These things are important, but they're only two of many possible factors that could be addressed. Optimum performance results from hiring the right people, training them in the right performance areas, enabling them with the right tools and knowledge, managing them well, and giving them opportunities to grow, while helping non-performers find more suitable employment. The chart below identifies some of the key variables that affect sales performance over the life cycle of a rep (see Figure 7C.1).

This is only a partial list, but it illustrates the point that choosing which levers to pull (that is, which KPIs or variables to strengthen) is not a simple task. Without some sort of guidance, you can waste a lot of time and energy trying to address every issue from hiring to exiting. Data analytics can pinpoint the major problem areas and the variables that provide the biggest leverage for change, so you can apply corrective actions judiciously and strategically instead of blindly and broadly.

A COACH IN YOUR CORNER

In this chapter, Cathie has instituted a performance coaching program for reps that augments her training classes. Because coaches focus primarily on individual rep success, they are the ideal complement to sales managers, who naturally tend to focus more on closing deals and making quota.

Hire/ Onboard Them	Train Them	Enable Them	Manage and Motivate Them	Grow/ Exit Them
Application of Predictive Analytics				
Which candidates are most likely to perform?	Which employees need training intervention?	Which prospects are highly likely to buy?	Which sales is person likely to miss his quota?	Which sales person is likely to leave?
Which candidates are most like to be high potential?	Which trainings are they most likely to benefit from?	What are the prospects most likely to buy?	What are the top competency issue?	Which retention strategy is most likely to work?
Which candidates are good fit for succession?	What is the likely impact of each of the training courses?	How much are they likely to spend at what price?	Which manager is most likely to perform?	Which reps have little future potential and needs to be exited?
Which candidates are fit for certain role type?		Who are they likely to buy from?	Which partner is most likely to perform?	Which candidates should be promoted as managers?
		When are they likely to buy?	Which sales channel is most likely to perform?	
		Which deals are most likely to close?	Predict quota attainment?	

Figure 7C.1 Sales Cycle of a Rep

By working with all reps on multiple levels of the organization, unimpeded by the walls of functional silos, performance coaches can help spot performance issues before they become major problems. Without breaking individual confidences, they can recommend corrective actions to increase the success of both the individual being coached and the organization.

Because their relationships with the people they coach are built on trust, coaches can be particularly helpful to a predictive analytics initiative, which also depends to a significant extent on trust. It takes a great deal of trust, for example, for reps to change longstanding behaviors based on the recommendations of a data analytics model rather than on their own intuition and experience. People are much more likely to accept and act on data-based input when they have a coach in their corner to reassure and encourage them.

Coaches can often pass on success-promoting ideas from one person they coach to another. This type of cross-pollination of best practices is one of the major advantages of organizational performance coaching. I strongly recommend performance coaching for any organization, and it can be especially valuable when data analytics is involved to guide and target development interventions.

DATA BUILDS CONFIDENCE AND MOTIVATION

This chapter also highlights the value of data analytics for building the confidence and motivation for sales reps. To a large extent, sales success starts in the mind. Before the results show up on the leader board, the confidence and motivation—indeed, even the "swagger"—must be present in the sales person. The individual rep, like Dumbo with the feather that gave him the ability to fly, must believe in the magic.

Sales people are like athletes. If they believe they can, they will. Those who are willing to put in an extraordinary level of effort and commitment will eventually get into the "zone," that mental space where they realize they're extraordinary.

Data analytics can help them get there. It is tremendously helpful when a coach or a manager can say to a rep who is falling short of quota, "I know you feel really discouraged now, but the people who tried this approach (took this class or rearranged their priorities in this way or focused on bundling Product A and E together when selling to big box retail in the Midwest) began to see extraordinary results. You can do it, too."

Such statements backed up by evidence in the form of data build confidence. Before-and-after data about the experiences of others instills hope, heightens motivation, improves morale, and promotes engagement. The typical reaction is for the recipient of this input to say, "Wow! That sounds like a solid idea. I'll give it a try." So much depends on attitude. Frequently, people's performance can start to improve even before the class or other corrective action begins simply because they know they are on the right

169

path and in an organization that will catch them before they fall and is committed to their success.

In our story, Cathie and her team motivated reps to jointly pursue accounts with partners by showing them that it works. Proof of success can enable reps to envision themselves following the same path and enjoying the same results.

Similarly, I've seen my own teams use success metrics to promote training courses. For example, rather than force new hires to complete on-boarding within a certain timeframe, we simply shared with them statistics that showed how recently hired reps who signed up for and completed sales boot camp within the first month on the job created more opportunities and closed more deals than colleagues who took the course in their second quarter on the job. You'd better believe those courses were full with reps who were all within their first four weeks on the job!

Sharing before-and-after business results for attendees of other courses has also prompted reps to sign up pretty quickly. Of course, it's not just about getting them to come to class. The goal is to make the reps and the company wildly successful, while at the same time improving the morale, motivation, engagement, and optimism of the company's culture.

Chapter 8

PRESCRIBING WHAT TO DO

As Hunter Cooke sat in his home office preparing for another day in the field, the stacks of unfinished travel reports and unpaid credit card bills that littered his desk mirrored the way he felt: scattered and out of control. It was already early August, and he was languishing in the bottom half of Trajectory's sales rep ranking.

His performance the year before had been miserable, too, but people had excused it because that was his first year with the company. He expected to do better this year—everyone expected him to do better—but so far he had only closed a few small deals. His manager was calling him practically every day telling him to get out of the office and make more calls. At one point Joe, the head of sales, also called him personally to give him an old school "win one for the Gipper" speech (not that Cooke knew who the Gipper was). That call just made him more depressed. Could it be that his superiors thought he was lazy? But if anything, Cooke was working too hard. He was racing around making so many calls that he felt like he was living one of those bad dreams he sometimes had, in which he was running as fast as he could but never getting anywhere.

It would have helped if all of the other reps were having the same problem, but Cooke had heard that a few of them were doing quite well. He was also aware of a new sense of excitement back at company headquarters in Palo Alto, and he was starting to resent the way those overly optimistic people in the corporate office meddled in his affairs. Cathie Martinez in enablement and Stacy Martin in sales operations, in particular, pestered him with emails trying to get him to take personalized trainings, build better relationships with partners, and things like that.

Hunter's wife entered the room with his morning cup of coffee just as he was finishing a phone call with his manager. She could tell that it had not gone well. It hurt her to see her husband so discouraged.

As she placed the coffee on his desk, she put her hand on his shoulder: "I believe in you, honey." Then she left the room. She had learned that it was best in these situations to give him space.

Hunter found himself looking at the picture of his family that he kept on his desk. He loved his family and hated being a poor provider. If he didn't start to get some traction by the end of the year, he'd have to start looking for another job.

Cooke checked his email again. It was mostly just the same old stuff. There was one from Cathie Martinez that he would have normally deleted, but the heading read "Congratulations!" so he decided to open it (see Figure 8.1).

"Who does this woman think she is? What makes her think she can sit in some headquarters building in another part of the country and know more about how I should do my job than I do?" Hunter's pride was about to make him snap. He picked up the phone and called Cathie to give her a piece of his mind.

When she answered the phone, Hunter ranted on about how bad the economy was and how he was not interested in being coached by someone who had probably never spent

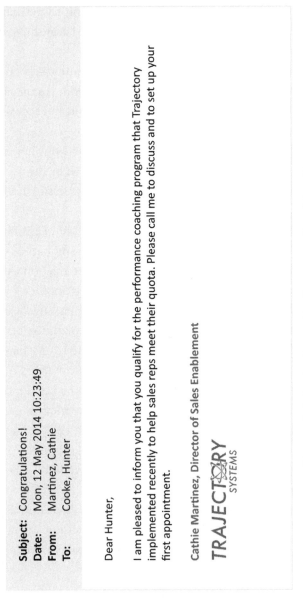

Subject: Congratulations!
Date: Mon, 12 May 2014 10:23:49
From: Martinez, Cathie
To: Cooke, Hunter

TRAJECT✷RY
SYSTEMS

Dear Hunter,

I am pleased to inform you that you qualify for the performance coaching program that Trajectory implemented recently to help sales reps meet their quota. Please call me to discuss and to set up your first appointment.

Cathie Martinez, Director of Sales Enablement

Figure 8.1 Invitation to Performance Coaching Program

a day selling in the field. To his surprise, Cathie didn't argue or defend herself. After a couple of minutes, Hunter was out of gas.

"I understand that you're frustrated," said Cathie, once Hunter had calmed down, "but let me show you some data that might help you make your quota this year."

Hunter laughed. "Data? How is data is going to help me?" asked Hunter. "What I need is better leads."

"Our data shows you're focusing on the wrong customers and partners," Cathie continued undaunted. "If you're willing to schedule a coaching appointment with me, I'll show you some things that will help you."

"That's my manager's job," said Hunter warily. "He's my supervisor. Tell him about it."

"Your manager knows about this program and supports it," replied Cathie. "He'll still be working with you to close deals. But we now have access to data and insights that allow us to coach you better."

"I'm too busy to add coaching appointments to my schedule," said Hunter, aware that he was starting to sound a bit petulant. He then apologized. "Look, I'm sorry, I know my numbers are down; I just need to get back out there and. ... "

Cathie cut him off. She'd seen the light and wanted to share the message. "Hunter, you only need to commit to the three one-hour phone calls, one week apart. If it goes well, you can decide to continue. Normally, I'd assign a coach to you, but if you're agreeable, I'll do it myself." There was a long pause. Cathie knew she had a convert. Then she added,

"I'll offer suggestions, but you're in the driver's seat. You call the shots. I'll be your coach, not your boss."

Hunter paused for a few seconds. "OK," said Hunter. "When do you want to schedule the first call? Next week?"

"Tomorrow at 8 a.m. your time," said Cathy. "We'll have a web conference. I'll send you an email with the call-in instructions. I look forward to talking with you."

As Hunter hung up the phone, he had mixed emotions—intimidated, embarrassed, and yet, he couldn't help being impressed by Cathie's desire to help him.

The next morning Cathie connected with Hunter by web conference. At first glance, it was exactly what he suspected. Charts, numbers, percentages, and all sort of corporate buzzwords. But as soon Cathie started explaining things, everything made sense. "We did some research using advanced analytics techniques to try to understand what differentiates above-average sales reps from below-average. This chart shows your performance with respect to the top drivers of attainment. We call these drivers KPIs, which is an acronym for key performance indicators" (see Figure 8.2).

"The top KPI tells us that your year-to-date bookings are low. Of course, you knew that."

"My manager reminds me of that every week," said Hunter, "and so does Stacy when she sends me my team ranking. Not to be rude, but if you think reminding me of how much I stink is going to inspire me, you can save your time."

Cathie laughed and clarified. "Hunter, my job is to help you find ways to meet your quota. I see you're above average when it comes to opportunity generation, and your

176

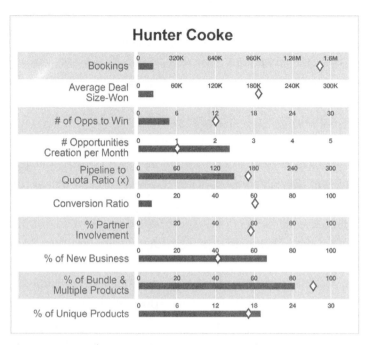

Figure 8.2 Hunter Cooke: Last Year's Performance

pipeline-to-quota ratio is pretty good," said Cathie. "That means you have been very busy."

"True, I'm always worried that you guys think I'm lazy because my win rate is so low," said Hunter.

"Well, this data says you are definitely not lazy. You've just been spending time on the wrong products and the wrong customers," continued Cathie. "This data shows that you're likely to meet quota if you make a few rather modest tweaks in your selling strategy."

"Tweaks? OK, let's tweak away," said Hunter.

"I'm not kidding," said Cathie with a laugh. "You have a good shot at making the year, and I'll show you how." Cathie referred to the chart that showed Hunter's deal size. "One of the top drivers of attainment is average deal size. That seems to be your biggest gap area. Our analysis shows that you need to close deals with an average deal size of $180K, while your current average deal size is $25K."

By now, Hunter was all in. "But how?"

"I have several recommendations" said Cathie, "but let's start with the simple ones. First, it doesn't appear that you're working with partners. Our top sales reps partner with the channel on 60 percent of their deals. Partner deals on average are six times larger than non-partner deals, and they have higher win rates."

"I don't know how to find good partners," said Hunter.

"I will give you a list of the top sales partners in your region, along with contact information for the channel sales managers," said Cathie. "This will also contain info on the performance of each of these partners with respect to average deal size."

"Very cool," agreed Hunter earnestly. "What else did you have in mind?"

"I recommend that you put more focus on product bundling to increase your deal size. More than 90 percent of the deals of successful reps are bundled. I'll send you a list of the top-selling product bundles that yield better-than-average deal sizes. I will also point you to pre-sales contacts and sales buddies who have successfully sold bundles and worked with partners, so you can talk with them and find out how they did it."

"That's awesome," said Hunter, truly impressed. "But why didn't my sales manager show me this crap before, instead of just giving me empty pep talks?"

"Actually, we didn't have this 'data' before. And we like to use the term data over 'crap,' just so you know," said Cathie. "Well, actually we had the data, we just didn't know how to use it. This is all new."

"OK, I'll give it a shot," said Hunter, "and we'll talk next week. But don't forget to send me the information you promised."

During the week, Hunter kept up his side of the bargain and implemented Cathie's suggestions. When it came time for their next call web conference, he was in a much better mood. In fact, they both had a laugh when Hunter said he was starving for some fresh "data." He was all ears, as Cathie relayed some new information. "By analyzing the approximately 23,000 deals that have been won, lost, or abandoned by all of the company's sales reps over the last two years, we have identified certain characteristics that are common to high-probability and low-probability deals. From that, we now have a model that can accurately provide the win probability for each of the sixteen deals in your pipe. Here's what our analysis of your pipe shows" (see Figure 8.3).

"The horizontal axis shows the expected closure dates, and the vertical axis shows the stages of the deals. Bigger bubbles mean bigger deal sizes, and darker bubbles mean there is a higher probability the deal will close. My recommendation is that you concentrate on the large dark, bubbles. Those are the high probability deals."

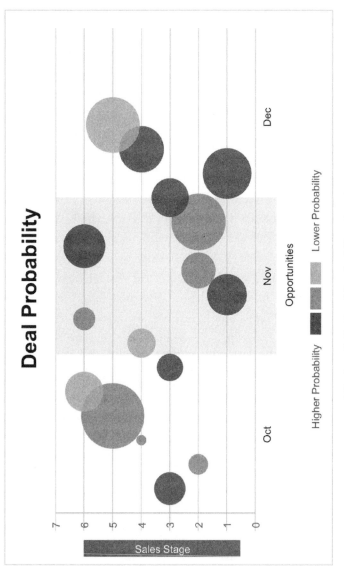

Figure 8.3 Deal Probability Scoring

"Big dark bubbles—good," said Hunter. "Little light bubbles, not good."

"Yes, but let's see why," Cathie continued. "Let's take a look at one of your lower probability deals to see why it's rated so low. This graphic shows the risk factors for this deal, ranked from top to bottom in descending order of impact" (see Figure 8.4).

"Your biggest risk indicator for this deal is that you've never closed a similar deal. This particular one involves a calibration solution for a healthcare provider, and my guess is you're not terribly experienced with the healthcare industry."

Hunter agreed: "I don't even know where my insurance card is—my wife handles all that."

"The data is right again," Cathie said with a laugh. "So looking down the chart, this product also has low win rates and is a single-product deal. Win rates of single-product deals average just 10 percent. Also, I notice that this deal is still in stage two, and the deal velocity indicates that it has not moved over the last five months. Finally, the low account win ratio indicates that you have not won many deals with this account in the past, mainly due to a strong competitive presence."

"I feel like you're clairvoyant." exclaimed Hunter, "but you can't ask me to just stop pursuing the leads I've been working on, even if they are low probability. It feels … risky."

"Managing by data instead of your gut instinct probably does seem risky," said Cathie. "And it's counterintuitive to everything you've learned about sales in your career, sort of like the pilot learning to fly an airplane by instruments rather than by sight. But give it a try. The riskiest thing is to

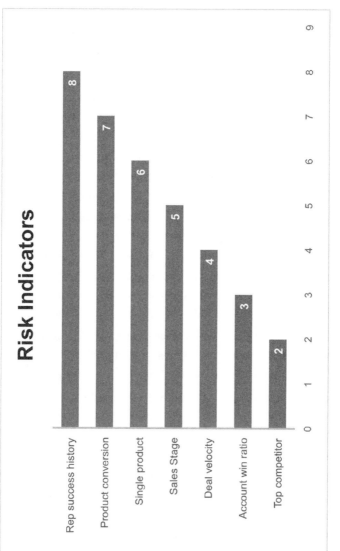

Figure 8.4 Risk Indicators

keep doing what you've been doing." This landed on Hunter. Cathie was right. She put up the next graphic "Recommended Next Steps" (see Figure 8.5).

"This is the recommended mitigation strategy for one of the deals in your pipeline," continued Cathie. "It's for a calibration module to the manufacturer of veterinary equipment and, in this particular sales situation, you're going up against one of our top competitors. That's the biggest risk factor, so you need to get out the competition's playbook and study up."

"Actually, I've never looked at the playbook," Hunter admitted. "I haven't had time."

"Tsk, tsk," said Cathie. "From here on out, that will be our secret. Why don't you pretend you're a pro quarterback just starting with a new team, and maybe you can get more excited about doing it."

"Not only are you going up against our biggest competitor, but I also notice that you've never had great success selling to this account," continued Cathie, "so I recommend that you meet with the senior management of the company to build relationships. And the velocity of this deal has been slow, so you should check to see whether there's a budget issue. If so, get permission for extra discounts in case you need them. I think the rest of the items on this strategy should be pretty self-explanatory."

"So you're going to give me a strategy for every one of the sixteen deals in my pipeline?" asked Hunter.

"Just for the top prospects," answered Cathie. "You can forget about the rest."

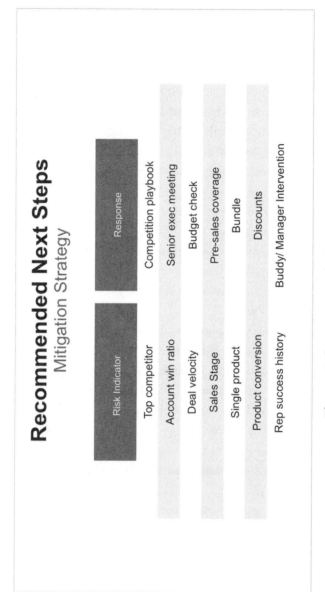

Figure 8.5 Recommended Next Steps

"How do I know what my top prospects are?" said Hunter. "More bubbles?"

"Yep, I'll get you your bubbles," said Cathie.

"Good. That takes care of deals," said Hunter, "but what about leads? Marketing sends me a bunch of leads that are worthless, then my manager accuses me of being lazy when I don't call on them. So I'm never sure if I should focus on closing the deals in the pipe or on going after more leads. Do you have anything that will help me prioritize that stuff?"

"This graphic will help," said Cathie. "It shows the propensity to buy of every one of your leads. The four quadrants correspond to the four industries you sell to. The bigger the rectangle, the bigger the potential order. And the darker the rectangle, the sooner the order is predicted to close" (see Figure 8.6).

"So I should go after the Healthlynx lead that's in the bottom right quadrant first?" asked Hunter. "It seems to have the highest probability of closing and the biggest dollar potential."

"You've got the idea," said Cathie. "Go after the high-probability leads and forget the rest. Do the same with your low-probability accounts. Forget about them."

"OK, but some of those accounts I've been hounding for months, so if I disappear they'll think they offended me."

Cathie thought about that for a moment, then said, "Don't be surprised if they send you a bottle of scotch to try and get back on your good side."

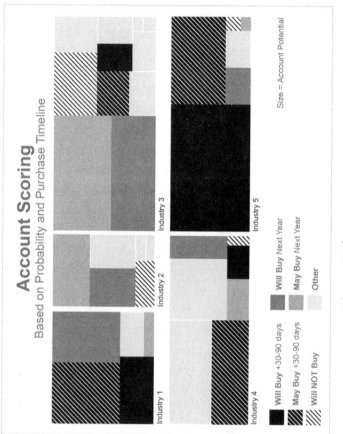

Figure 8.6 Account Scoring

Hunter laughed and said that if that happened, he would include that in his data. They had a big laugh out of that one. After he hung up the phone, Hunter realized that this was the first time he had laughed in weeks.

SUMMARY

Hunter Cooke, a sales rep in his second year with Trajectory, is turning in yet another poor performance. He's rushing around trying to close deals, but nothing seems to click. Unless things change, he will fall far short of making his annual quota. The stress of his lack of success is hurting his morale, his family life, and probably his health. He feels he gets no support from his regional sales manager, and he regards the sales people back at the company's headquarters as nuisances.

One day Cathie Martinez, head of enablement, contacts Hunter and offers to coach him using analytics. At first Hunter is annoyed, but ultimately he agrees. Cathie shows him some data that amazes him. Working from the data and following Cathie's suggestions, Hunter starts to better focus his efforts.

COMMENTARY

We began in Chapter 1 by looking at analytics at a very high level. That's the natural place to start. As we have progressed through the book, we've gradually drilled down in ever-tightening concentric circles, until at last we have arrived at the individual level.

The Holy Grail of data analytics, at least with respect to sales, is to increase the effectiveness of the individual. When individuals are more productive, motivated, engaged, and happy, the organization will be more successful. The real power comes when big data gets personal.

No one wants to waste time and effort doing work that's ineffective. People want to produce positive results that promote the success of the organization. When properly offered, people welcome suggestions about how they can perform better. They don't want the corporation to be "Big Brother" and try to tell them what to do and what not to do in every area of their lives. But they do like it when an organization says something like the following:

"You have untapped potential we would like to help you develop so you can be even more successful. If you are interested, we will give you some clear guidelines based on objective data about how you can take your performance to the next level. Our intention is not to invade your privacy or tell you how to run your life, but simply to help you, and ultimately the organization, be more effective."

I believe offering this kind of support is one of the key responsibilities of the corporation. But it needs to be done in the right way. People don't like surprises. I would never suggest that you try to trick people or do something on the sly. The corporation should have really clear policies about its intentions and practices regarding analytics, especially with respect to prescriptive analytics.

Your bottom-line motivation with data analytics should be to help people. If you accomplish that, you will automatically be helping the organization. If a company is very up-front and transparent about what it is doing, and if it starts with a foundation built on mutual trust between employees and management, data analytics will work. If management, on the other hand, has broken trust with employees in the past by rolling out programs under false pretenses, employees may justifiably be skeptical about data analytics.

This is why a performance coaching program within the organization can be so important. The suggestions offered as a result of prescriptive analytics need to be delivered through relationships built on trust and in ways that engender trust. Just as people need to be able to trust the pharmacist who gives them their medical prescriptions, employees need to be able to trust the organizational leaders who give them an analytics prescription.

ABOUT PRESCRIPTIVE ANALYTICS

Explanation: Prescriptive analytics is the logical extension of the first three analytics stages: descriptive analytics, diagnostic analytics, and predictive analytics. Once you understand the deeper processes that underlie your data (descriptive analytics), have a sense of why they are happening (diagnostic analytics), and have predictions about the future (predictive analytics), the next step is to act on your knowledge. That's where prescriptive analytics comes in. It produces insights and actions intended to improve future outcomes.

Example: In this chapter, the prescriptive analytics is presented in the form of personalized recommendations for Hunter Cooke, who is struggling to meet his quota. Here are some specific examples:

1. The first chart that Cathie shows to Hunter identifies the top KPIs that are important for quota attainment. As you may recall, the team found out which KPIs were most important using diagnostic analytics in Chapter 6. They also determined what values top attainers had for each of these KPIs. To help Hunter understand where he might be weak, Cathie showed him how his KPI values stacked up against the top attainers.

2. Using probabilistic predictive models trained on historical data on deals, Henry and Jennifer built a model that was able to generate the probability that a deal will close. The results of these predictions for upcoming deals were summarized for Hunter in the second chart (Figure 8.3). This allowed him to focus his attention on the deals most likely to close.

3. Next, the team turned its attention to the deals that had a low probability of closing. Using diagnostic analytics approaches, they determined which KPIs should be included in a predictive deal model, and they developed

a KPI profile for high-probability deals. Using these profiles, they generated a ranked list of the KPIs that were lagging for each of the deals in Hunter's pipeline. These results, which are shown for one deal in the third chart (Figure 8.4), provided Hunter with specific guidance about what actions to take with respect to particular low probability deals.

Insight: Prescriptive analytics is the least established of the four types of analytics because each company has very different needs. Predictive analytics models, on the other hand, have very similar structures, no matter what the domain. When given some input X, their output should be Y. When given 10,000 examples of X and Y pairs, they will learn a mathematical relationship between the two.

But no analogous simple summary applies to prescriptive analytics. Effective prescriptions are more than just an analytics concern; they are a collaborative effort between the analyst and the business expert who has a deep understanding of what information the company, its employees, and its customers need. The two must work together to find the best way to leverage and extend the work that was done during the descriptive, diagnostic, and predictive analytics stages.

A SALES PERSON'S MENTAL MODEL
Prescriptive analytics can produce many actionable recommendations, although prioritizing them can be difficult.

One approach is to think like a sales person and consider the decisions that must be made each day.

This thinking process is illustrated by the mental model below (Figure 8C.1). Every new sales rep needs to decide which accounts in the territory to pursue, what specific products to sell, which specific prospects (people) to reach out to, and what sales approach to use.

Account prioritization logic can help prioritize the list based on propensity to buy, purchase timeline, and account potential. Similarly, product predictor algorithms can suggest the best product fit based on product affinity analysis, whitespaces, and identified business issues.

LinkedIn and contact databases are great tools to identify business contacts that are heavily used by the sales community. They provide the valuable ability to choose the right contact profile and reach out with targeted messages. Sales reps can save considerable desk time by using these types of simple contact-based and person-based recommendation systems. Intelligent sales playbooks, which recommend what to do in specific sales situations, can also be invaluable, especially for new sales reps who desire to ramp up quickly.

Advanced analytics is not appropriate for every situation. Sales reps are not analysts, and most of them are not particularly interested in graphs and charts. They are looking for actionable next steps that will help them achieve their sales goals.

It's up to sales leadership to provide the support systems to give reps those actionable next steps.

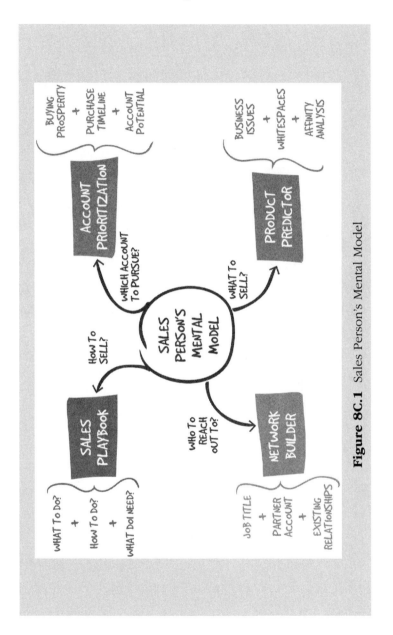

Figure 8C.1 Sales Person's Mental Model

Chapter 9

CELEBRATING SUCCESS

Entering the conference room to start the first sales review meeting of the new year, Pam noticed something strange: her sales leadership team was already there. It wasn't like them to all be on time for a meeting. Then, two other things caught her eye: a large cake and the ridiculous, multi-colored paper hat that Raj wore whenever anyone at Trajectory had a birthday celebration. "OK, who's birthday did I forget?" Pam asked, as she set down her bag.

"Ours," said Stacy. "Exactly one year ago today, you told us we were going to try data analytics, and most of us thought you were crazy. And now we have reason to celebrate. We're one!"

Pam smiled, shook her head, and looked over the group. She felt a closeness to them that can only come from fighting battles together. Stacy Martin, Cathie Martinez, Raj Kapoor, Barbara Acres, and Andy Mahoney had all been present at that contentious "blame game" meeting a year before. Jim Forrester, now VP of North America Sales, and Henry Crawford, who now provided consulting services to Trajectory and several other clients, had joined the team a short time later. Today, Jennifer Chan, although she had only been with the group a month, fit in so well that she was regarded as a full-fledged member.

Pam thought back to that day at the Dallas airport when, all alone, she first began to chart sales KPIs. Now, twelve months later, Trajectory had stopped its downward slide and was well on its way to recovery. The past year had been an arduous, perilous climb up a largely unmapped mountain. She was overwhelmed with pride.

After most of the cake had disappeared, Pam started the meeting. "Some of you weren't at that sales review meeting a year ago, but I can assure you that this meeting is a lot more fun." Several people chuckled. Pam continued: "I'm so proud of what we've accomplished. Back then it was 'management by guesstimate,' but now we know that's just for amateurs."

Pam continued: "Stacy, congratulations on transforming your group into a world-class data analytics team. I'd like you to come up here and lead the meeting."

Stacy made her way to the front of the room. "Thanks, Pam. I have several slides to show everyone that summarize our results for this past year compared to the year before. I think you'll find them encouraging." She projected a slide onto the white board (see Figure 9.1).

"As you can see, our bookings increased by 38 percent, our attainment percentage increased from 83 percent to 106 percent, and the percentage of reps meeting quota increased from 20 percent to 60 percent. Also, notice that the average sales per rep figure. ... "

Suddenly, Stacy stopped talking and stared over everyone's heads toward the doorway behind them. Pam wondered what was going on, then turned to see what had captured Stacy's attention. Standing in the doorway was Trajectory's CEO, David Craig.

"I heard there was going to be an interesting meeting today, and I thought I'd stop by," David said with a smile. "And now that I see that there's cake—I'm not going anywhere."

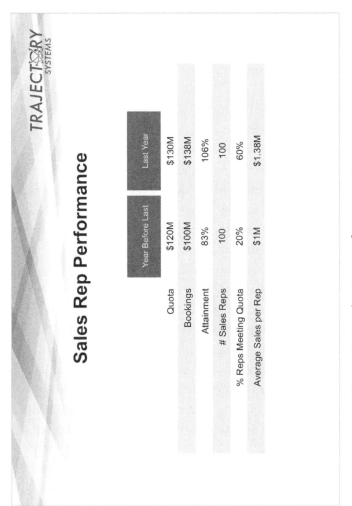

Figure 9.1 Sales Rep Performance Overview

"Glad you could make it, David," Pam said. "Stacy is walking us through some reports on this past year. We're happy to share everything with you," said Pam, cutting the big boss a piece of cake, "including our cake."

Stacy continued by putting up a second slide, titled "KPI Improvements" (see Figure 9.2). "As you can see, the number of abandoned deals has dropped from 38 percent to 29 percent during the past year," she explained. "Opportunities generated per month per rep has doubled, and our win rate has improved from 45 to 59 percent. Partner engagement has also increased."

"Sweet, I'm loving those numbers!" exclaimed Craig.

"It gets better," said Stacy, pulling up another slide. "Look at how the entire rep performance curve has clearly shifted to the right" (see Figure 9.3).

"How?" David Craig asked, as he wiped a crumb off his Hugo Boss suit.

"We're planning to do a deep dive of the process steps for you and the key Trajectory leaders," said Pam.

"Our data-based performance coaching program has been key to turning the ship around," said Cathie, jumping in. "To supplement our analytics capabilities, I put together a team of four performance coaches who work with the newest sales reps. They check in with the reps every week and walk them through improvement opportunities uncovered by prescriptive analytics. For the rest of the sales people, we've coached their managers on how to use the data and information to drive improvement for their teams."

"How do you use prescriptive analytics?" queried Craig. He knew the answer to his question before he asked it.

TRAJECTORY SYSTEMS

Team Average

	Year Before Last	Last Year
# unique products sold	8	10
% partner engagement	46%	57%
Median deal size	$20,000	$65,000
Opportunities generated per quarter	2	4
% abandoned deals	38%	29%
% bundled deals	26%	44%
Win rate	45%	59%
% upsell deals in pipeline	50%	38%
Account size (# users)	2,500	7,500

Figure 9.2 Sales Rep Performance Overview (Team Average)

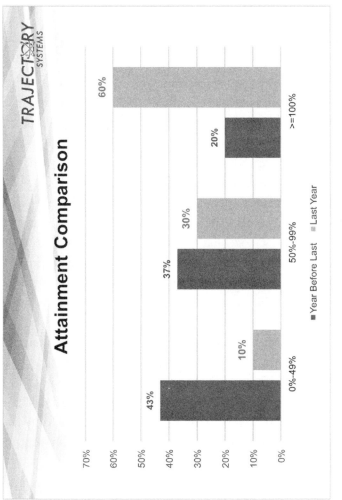

Figure 9.3 Attainment Distribution Comparison

But by asking, David Craig was giving Pam's team the space to show what they'd learned and how they'd changed.

"Essentially, insights and recommended actions derived from analytical data that improve future outcomes," answered Pam. "Our coaches provide insights and suggest actions to the reps, and the reps make the decisions about what to do with the information. Prescriptive analytics can be very helpful at the organizational level, and it is especially powerful when delivered from a coach or a manager to a rep on a one-to-one basis."

"Seems pretty labor-intensive," said Craig. "How long are we implementing this for?"

"We'll continue the one-on-one coaching program until all the sales managers are up to speed with data analytics and capable of coaching their reps using the dashboard," answered Cathie. "It's a very people-intensive approach, which has been appropriate given the dire situation we were in. But when things are back on track, we plan to transition from a high-touch to a high-tech approach."

"What dashboard are you talking about?" asked Craig.

"We built a personal recommendation dashboard," said Pam. "We wanted all of the reps to be able to view their gap areas, the recommendations they have received, and the progress they have made to close their gaps. The performance coaches have shortlisted at-risk performers to counsel and coach them."

"I'm impressed!" exclaimed David. "What are you calling this program?"

"We don't have a name for it," said Pam. "It's just data analytics applied to sales."

"Well, some of us actually did come up with a name," said Stacy, smiling. "We call this system PAM."

Pam looked puzzled: "Pam?"

"Yes," said Stacy with a broad smile. "PAM is an acronym for *Prescriptive Action Model*." Pam was both honored and embarrassed. She could only laugh.

"Well, I'd like to feature both PAMs at our annual sales conference at the end of this month," said David. "This is very exciting."

"The most exciting part to me is the positive impact data analytics can have on the lives of individuals," said Pam. "Cathie, tell David about Hunter Cooke."

"Hunter had been with the company about a year and a half when I started coaching him in early August, as part of our performance coaching program," said Cathie. "He was resistant at first and pessimistic, because for some time he had been near the bottom of our national leader board."

"He fit the typical profile of a bottom performer that we felt we could really turn around. Smart, energetic, but just didn't have the tools," added Pam.

"When I showed Hunter the data on how he could get a greater return on his efforts, he followed the suggestions I gave him," continued Cathie. "Or maybe I should say that he followed the suggestions that the data gave us both. Within three months, he had pared his list of twenty-seven leads down to the top eight. Out of those, he created six large-size opportunities and closed four of them before year-end. He started working with partners on virtually all of his deals, and his average deal size went up from about $25,000 to $100,000."

"It's the turnaround story of the year," added Pam. "No one thought he was going to make his annual quota, including Hunter himself, but he did, and now he's in the top quartile in terms of sales attainment. But the real story is not just in the numbers. Cathie, read Hunter's email."

Cathie read from her laptop screen:

"I'm writing to thank you for coaching me these past few months. When you first contacted me, I had just about given up on making it at Trajectory and was getting ready to go. I felt like a real failure in the eyes of my family, and in many ways I was. I let my problems at work spill over into my family life. I was in a very dark place. In fact, I want to apologize for how rude I was when we first started working together. Thanks for not losing patience with me.

I consider it something of a miracle that I made quota this year. The data you shared with me, coupled with your wise counsel, made all the difference. I am truly grateful to be part of such a great company and to have you in my corner as my coach. If I can ever return the favor, please let me know.

Most sincerely,

Hunter Cooke

"That's magnificent! We've got to get Hunter to say a few words at the sales kickoff meeting in Scottsdale later this month," said David. "His story will be a real encouragement to the other reps."

"I'll ask him to share his story," said Pam. "Let's give him the royal treatment. He lives in San Diego. We can fly him to Scottsdale first class."

"I have a better idea," said Jim. "San Diego's on the way to Scottsdale. Let's have Henry pick him up and deliver him to the front door of the convention center in his Spyder!" Henry looked up. Normally he didn't like taking the Spyder on long trips, but considering that the Del Mar race track was on the way to San Diego, he said, "Sure, sounds fun."

■ ■ ■

"Thanks for meeting me, Pam." Joe Kirsh stood up and put out his hand when she approached the lunch table.

"Of course, Joe. Your voice mail sounded urgent. What's going on?" They shook hands before Pam sat and spread the linen napkin across her lap and had a sip of her San Pellegrino.

"I'm going to be straight with you, Pam," Joe said, "I was on the wrong side of how things played out at Trajectory. I've got to get with the new program." Joe leaned in a bit as he lowered his voice, "The Milleniums are taking over."

"You mean Millennials?" Pam asked with a smile.

"Yes, that's what they're called," Joe said, looking around the restaurant to see who might be listening. "They're whip-smart and not easily impressed or intimidated, so I'm not sure how to interact with them. I'm too young to retire for good, so maybe we could work out a deal. You tutor me a bit on that data stuff you're driving and I can get you discounts on bulk pharmaceutical purchases from my new company."

"Or, how about I help get you up to speed on how you can apply data analytics in your industry? You keep the sacks of drugs, but your team and my team work side by side at our Day of Service event next month. It will be really satisfying to spend a day repairing stadium benches at the local middle school." Pam smiled as she looked at her menu.

"Will there be any Millennials there?" Joe asked with a furrowed brow.

Pam nodded, "Yes, probably. But you'll be among friends."

SUMMARY

As Pam and her team meet for the first sales review meeting of the new year, on the anniversary of the infamous "blame game" meeting, the mood is upbeat. The year has ended well, and Pam is proud of the results her people have delivered. David Craig, Trajectory's CEO, unexpectedly shows up and is very impressed by the reports Stacy presents highlighting their progress for the year. The company's sales function has clearly turned the corner.

A highlight of the meeting occurs when Cathie reads an email from sales rep Hunter Cooke about how prescriptive analytics, coupled with performance coaching, turned around his sales performance, and indeed his life. When Craig asks whether they have given a name to the set of analytics methodologies they have applied to sales, Stacy answers that they have named them "PAM." Pam Sharp is taken aback, until Stacy explains that PAM is an acronym for Predictive Action Model. As the meeting adjourns, Craig indicates to Pam that her success at Trajectory has put her in line for a promotion.

SUMMARY OF THE PAM PROCESS

In the story, David Craig asks Pam to explain how PAM works. She replies that she would be happy to prepare a special presentation for him and suggests that possibly some of the other company leaders would like to attend as well. But you don't have to wait. You are about to be treated to a key portion of that special presentation.

The four steps of the Predictive Action Model that Pam and her team developed over the course of a year are summarized in both text and graphic form below. I hope this information will be helpful to you as a reference tool.

1. Collect Sales Rep Data
   - Brainstorm all the variables that drive sales rep success. These are often called key performance indicators (KPIs). The Trajectory simulation considered 137 variables.
   - Collect as many variables (KPIs) as you can.
   - Gather metrics. For example, from your HRIS, gather the number of years the rep has been with the

company, and the number of years the rep has been in sales. From the CRM, gather the rep's average deal size and the rep's typical product mix.

2. Analyze the Data

- Use statistical techniques to understand what differentiates above-average performers from average and below-average performers. Pam and her team divided reps into three attainment groups: bottom, middle, and top.

- Perform two types of analyses: (1) *descriptive* analytics, to gather intuitive input about how the KPIs are related to attainment, and (2) *diagnostic* analytics, to determine which KPIs are most important to attainment.

- Use the top KPIs and different rep groups (top, middle, and bottom) to come up with profiles of performers. Use these profiles to help set KPI benchmarks. (This helps identify which metrics are the major predictors of success in order of priority. From this information, models can be built that will predict what attainment group each rep will fall into.)

- Analyze the performance of each sales rep against these metrics to identify gap areas and suggested personalized enablement plans.

3. Forecast Performance

- Measure past sales rep performance against goals to train your model to predict which reps will not meet their quotas. This helps create a shortlist of reps to focus on.

- Test the outcome of the predictions for accuracy to modify the model as needed.
- Apply the same techniques to identify which deals may or may not close, and which prospects may or may not buy.

4. Recommend Action
- After identifying gap areas through a trained model, make recommendations to each rep. For example, recommendations might include (1) which products to focus on, (2) what percentage of the pipeline should have partner engagement, (3) what percentage of the pipeline should be generated via bundled product deals, (4) how much focus to put on new business, (5) which training courses to attend, etc.
- Create personalized action plans and coach reps to understand the data and follow the recommendations. In the story, we prescribed individual targets for each of the top KPIs for each sales rep.
- Gain insights to improve sales operations, product development, lead generation, and other activities. Opportunities for continuous improvement exist in all groups that support sales.

Prescriptive Action Model

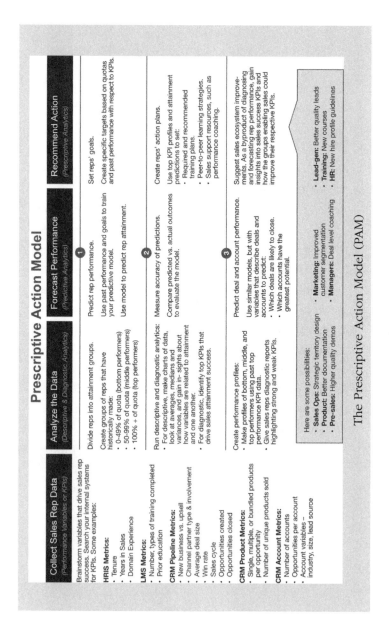

Collect Sales Rep Data (Performance Variables or KPIs)	Analyze the Data (Descriptive & Diagnostic Analytics)	Forecast Performance (Predictive Analytics)	Recommend Action (Prescriptive Analytics)
Brainstorm variables that drive sales rep success. Search your internal systems for KPIs. Some examples:	Divide reps into attainment groups.	Predict rep performance.	Set reps' goals.
	Create groups of reps that have historically made:	Use past performance and goals to train your predictive model.	Create specific targets based on quotas and past performance with respect to KPIs.
HRIS Metrics: • Tenure • Years in Sales • Domain Experience	• 0-49% of quota (bottom performers) • 50-99% of quota (middle performers) • 100% + of quota (top performers)	Use model to predict rep attainment.	
LMS Metrics: • Number, types of training completed • Prior education	Run descriptive and diagnostic analytics:	Measure accuracy of predictions.	Create reps' action plans.
CRM Pipeline Metrics: • New business vs. upsell • Channel partner type & involvement • Average deal size • Win rate • Sales cycle • Opportunities created • Opportunities closed	• For descriptive, make charts of data, look at averages, medians and variances, and gain in- sights about how variables are related to attainment and one another. • For diagnostic, identify top KPIs that drive sales attainment success.	Compare predicted vs. actual outcomes to evaluate the model.	Use top KPI profiles and attainment predictions to set: • Required and recommended training plans. • Peer-to-peer learning strategies. • Sales support resources, such as performance coaching.
CRM Product Metrics: • Single, multiple, or bundled products per opportunity • Number of unique products sold	Create performance profiles:	Predict deal and account performance.	Suggest sales ecosystem improvements. As a byproduct of diagnosing and forecasting rep performance, gain insights into sales success KPIs and how the groups enabling sales could improve their respective KPIs.
CRM Account Metrics: • Number of accounts • Opportunities per account • Account variables – industry, size, lead source	• Make profiles of bottom, middle, and top performers using past top performance KPI data. • Give sales reps diagnostic reports highlighting strong and weak KPIs.	Use similar models, but with variables that describe deals and accounts to predict: • Which deals are likely to close. • Which accounts have the greatest potential.	
	Here are some possibilities: • **Sales Ops:** Strategic territory design • **Product:** Better documentation • **Pre-sales:** Higher quality demos	• **Marketing:** Improved customer segmentation • **Managers:** Deal level coaching	• **Lead-gen:** Better quality leads • **Training:** New courses • **HR:** New hire profile guidelines

The Prescriptive Action Model (PAM)

ABOUT THE AUTHOR

Jenny Dearborn is one of the world's leading authorities on sales enablement, training, and learning, with special expertise in utilizing big data and predictive analytics to improve sales effectiveness. As senior vice president and chief learning officer at SAP, she designs, aligns, and drives employee learning and enablement strategy and programs for the company's approximately 68,000 employees around the globe. Jenny is recognized as one of the 50 Most Powerful Women in Technology by the National Diversity Council. Her team was named the number 1 top performing corporate learning organization in 2013 by *Elearning Magazine*. Although she has deep roots in Silicon Valley, with degrees from UC Berkeley, San Jose State, and Stanford University, she has a strong focus in international business and has traveled extensively in her career and, through the Fortune Most Powerful Women Network, she is a mentor for the U.S. State Department to female entrepreneurs in developing countries. She writes and speaks extensively and is a sought-after keynoter for industry and corporate events. She lives with her family in Palo Alto, California.

Index

Individual names in italics indicate a fictional employee of the fictional Trajectory Systems.

Data analytics *(continued)*
using, 28–41, 42–44; as the
real game-changer, 115–116;
sales reps performance, 5, 7,
9, 14; value for building
sales reps confidence and
motivation, 168–170. *See also*
Big Data

Data analytics application
examples: basketball coach
to game preparation, 32–33;
Moneyball (film) on Oakland
A's experience with, 107;
pilot guiding the airplane,
33–34; practical change
management, 116–118;
training programs, 115–116.
See also Data analytics
programs

Data analytics capability: the
steps toward increasing,
62–67; strategizing to build
your, 61–62

Data analytics capability-
building: be careful when
selecting a consultant for,
65; do seek expertise for,
64–65; don't rush to
outsource data analytics,
63–64; learning to ask the
right questions for, 65–66;
transparency and trust for,

66; understand that software
isn't a magic bullet, 64

Data analytics models: black
box model on KPIs, 163–
164; developed for Trajectory
sales force, 56–58, 59; for
horseracing, 57. *See also* PAM
(Prescriptive Action Model)

Data analytics programs:
benefits of having a successful, 67; "internal terrorists"
that try to sabotage, 117;
securing buy-ins from
everyone involved, 117–118.
See also Data analytics
application examples

Data analytics taskforce:
celebrating success,
196–207; descriptive
analytics report made by,
96–112; KPIs performance
diagnostic analysis report
made by, 124–139;
prioritizing areas for reps
help using predictive
analytics, 146–165; *Stacy's*
wiki of notes and action
items, 146–147; Total Sales
Rep Bookings KPI map
development by the, 34, 35,
73, 80–86. *See also specific
taskforce member*

Performance coaching: applying predictive analytics to, 147, 158–159, 161; *Joe Kirsch* asking *Pam* for, 204, 206; prescriptive analytics applied to, 172–190; training programs augmented by, 166, 168; on understanding and using KPIs, 177–186, 189–190

Performance coaching program: on account scoring, 184, 185; on deal probability scoring, 179–180; following *Hunter Cooke* through the process of, 172–187, 190; *Hunter Cooke's* feedback letter on the, 205, 207; invitation to the, 174; on mitigation strategy for deal in your pipeline, 182–184; on risk indicators, 181–182; on securing partner involvement, 178. *See also* Learning programs

Person-based recommendation system, 192

Pipeline performance: coaching program on mitigation strategy for, 182–184; diagnostic analytics

to prove business impact on, 143; Number of sales rep bookings pipeline KPI map, 34, 73; overview of sales rep, 9; sales rep bookings pipeline, 34, 35, 38–39, 73, 96–98; total sales rep bookings KPI, 35, 38–39, 73

Playing blame game: explaining the poor sales performance by, 4–17; illustration of the roles taken when, 14

Predictive analytics: applied to improve sales rep performance, 166; applied to KPI improvements, 148; deal size growth, 150; definition of, 46–47, 162; *Henry's* black box model on KPIs for, 163–164; in relation to three other types of analytics, 45; PAM model on using, 209; prior year attainment distribution, 155; prioritizing areas for reps help using, 146–165; Rep Attainment Distribution, 105–106, 156; similarities of tools for diagnostic analytics and, 164–165; there are no